The Bells Are Not Silent

Stories of Church Bells in China

by Joann Pittman

Sue,

May you be blessed by these
stories of God's faithfulness
to His church in China

Joann

FOREWORD BY NOËL PIPER

The Bells Are Not Silent: Stories of Church Bells in China
by Joann Pittman

About the author:
Joann went to China in 1984 to teach English for one year, and ended up staying for twenty-eight years. During her time in China she lived in three different cities (Zhengzhou, Changchun, and Beijing) and worked as a teacher, program director, language learning coach, and cross-cultural trainer. She has also served as adjunct faculty at the University of Northwestern (MN), Wheaton College (IL), and Taylor University (IN) , teaching courses in Chinese history, contemporary society, and Chinese language. She is fluent in Mandarin Chinese and is the author of Survival Chinese Lessons. Joann is currently the Senior Vice President at ChinaSource. Her blog "Outside-In" can be found at www.joann-pittman.com.

Edited by Julia Christianson
Book design by Andy Bruner
Cover design by Chloe Sng

First Edition

ISBN 978-1541051102 (paperback)
ISBN 978-0-9981403-1-5 (ebook)

Printed in the United States of America.

Contents

Foreword
by Noël Piper

According to Webster's Dictionary, serendipity is "finding valuable or pleasant things that are not looked for."

When someone asks my favorite word, that's the answer: serendipity. My attention is caught first by the sound of the word—seren-dipity. It begins serenely, like a rider on a sedate steed following a well-planned route. Then without warning, the word breaks into a rapid gallop toward an unexpected destination where something wonderful waits. The word actually sounds like what it is.

As Joann says, she didn't set out looking for bells when she and I traveled to Sichuan. Joann had created an itinerary for us that included transportation by Chinese riverboat, train, plane, car, and high-speed magnetic levitation train (maglev) to visit certain places on certain days. Joann was the guide, networker, and translator. I was the researcher, seeking background, atmosphere, and details for the book I was writing.

Then about a week and a half along our well-planned path, we visited the church that was on the schedule for that day. Our discovery of the bell in that church's tower was Joann's hour of serendipity. Since then, at the slightest mention of any bell her eyes light up.

That first bell and the pastor's comment about its survival were fascinating, a parable of the church in China. The significance would have ended there for me. But it didn't for Joann. The bells' stories stirred her to set out on a quest for church bells elsewhere in China.

It is difficult for us outsiders to grasp the complexities of Christianity in China. But perhaps the bells in this book can help. Each has a story that is a glimpse into some piece of the history of God's work that has significance in China and beyond.

Introduction

I didn't start by looking for the bells. The opportunity came, as so many things in China and life do, from a relationship, a commitment to mutual assistance. Once that opportunity landed and took root in my love of observation and searching for stories in obscure places and encounters, I was hooked.

"We have an old bell in our steeple," the pastor of a Chinese church said to me. "It has some English writing on it, but we can't read it. Can you help us?"

That bell, it turned out, was a 126-year-old bell that had been cast in the United States. The pastor told us what little he knew about the bell and how it came to be hanging in his church after surviving more than a century of war, revolution, and political chaos. The story that unfolded was more than the story of a bell; it was a testament to God's sustaining grace to his church in China through difficult times.

I made the discovery of that first bell while on a trip with Noël Piper, a dear friend and the wife of my pastor at Bethlehem Baptist Church in Minneapolis. We were in Sichuan Province doing

3

research on Esther Nelson, a woman who had been sent out as a missionary to China from the church, then named the First Swedish Baptist Church in the 1920's.

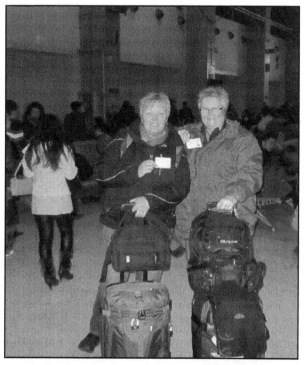

Joann and Noël setting out on their "Esther Expedition"

During renovations at the church Noël had stumbled upon a box of letters that Esther had sent to Elsie Viren, the church secretary and Esther's best friend. As she read the letters, Noël was gripped by the story of this woman who seemed to have been forgotten by everyone except by a few very old people in our church.

When Noël visited China in 2009, I had already lived in the country for more than twenty years. During her stay with me at my home in Beijing, she shared the story of Esther and the letters and told me of her dream to one day travel to Sichuan to visit the places where Esther had lived and worked. Knowing that I shared her love of history and adventure, she asked if I would be willing to go along as her guide and translator. Without stopping to think about it for even a second, I agreed, and thus what we dubbed "The Esther Expedition" was born. Writing just prior to the trip in March of 2012, Noël introduced Esther and our journey to her blog readers:

> *Through visiting places Esther lived and following routes she traveled—in particular that last journey wrenching her from her beloved land and people—we want to understand her life, place and people from a perspective closer to her experience. As she wrote: "I cannot explain how happy I am to be going up this river once again. There is something that takes ahold of me, thrills me, as I go inward. It cannot be explained, it can only be experienced."*[1]

Our unexpected discovery of the bell was made in the largest Protestant church in Yibin, Sichuan, the one in which Esther Nelson worshipped when she lived there in the 1940's.

After seeing the bell and hearing its story, it dawned on me that if there was an old bell hanging in a church in a remote city of Sichuan Province, then there must be other bells scattered all over the country with similar stories.

In the year after we discovered the first bell, I travelled to Harbin, Qingdao, Tianjin, and scoured the churches in Beijing, my adopted hometown, in search of more. On my journey I found bells from Russia, Germany, and France.

The bells that I found were all cast during what was still the heyday of church bells, when a steeple and bell were considered

---

1. Noël Piper, "Our Following in the Footsteps Expedition," Tell Me When to Pack, (November 2011): http://www.tellmewhentopack.com/2011/11/our-following-in-the-footsteps-expedition/

essential elements of church architecture and worship. Not only had someone arranged for the bells to be cast, and invested what must have been a considerable sum of money, but they were also deemed important enough to transport to the other side of the world. In other words, as churches and mission boards planned their China missionary endeavors, getting a bell to China was obviously a priority. To modern missionaries, who have moved away from valuing those elements of ritual and tradition in favor of simplicity and localization, this is an almost inconceivable notion.

But why, in a country that has experienced both anti-Christian and anti-Western convulsions, do these bells still peal? Why keep that tradition alive? Why are they not silent? Perhaps the answer can be found in a conversation I had with a Chinese pastor about the prevalence of Western hymns in the Chinese church. Pointing out to her that so many churches in the West, particularly in the United States, are abandoning the "old" hymns, I asked her why they are still being sung in Chinese churches. Her response to me was that singing the great hymns of the church, even though they were foreign, helped the Chinese church tether itself to the Church Universal, to the Global Body of Christ, even though political barriers have been erected to keep it separate.

Modern church planters may not be able to imagine taking a bell to the field; however a small article in a 19th-century catalogue for the Brosamer Bell Foundry clearly spells out the value of church bells:

Many of our feeble churches, now without a bell, would use every effort to procure one, did they fully appreciate its value as a church help. The church is nothing except it gather together the people within its walls; and no material agency effects this assemblage so much as a bell on the church. Its first ringing on Sunday morning announces to the people that service is surely set for that day. It stirs them up to make ready and be in season when the worship begins. It serves as a general invitation to all within hearing to come to the house of God.

Introduction

Each one feels himself solicited by its loud calls. The stranger who has just entered the place to settle, and the stranger stopping at the hotel, as well as the members of the church, count themselves welcomed by its cordial tones.

The bell also serves to awaken the consciences of some in whom the habit of church-going has become weak. To those who do not know the location of the church, it declares the way; to those who would forget the hour of service it points the time. It is, in fact, the general voice of mother church herself, to the world without, exhorting it to attend her courts.

There is many a country church whose half-empty seats are largely owing to the want of a bell to declare its existence and locality. There are many struggling congregations whose weakness and troubles would quickly disappear, if they would raise a bell to ring the mass of the people together. For want of such a proclamation, the world often knows nothing either of the church's presence or its place.

All the people in any town have an interest in owning a church bell. They need it for funerals and weddings, for days of rejoicing and for national celebrations. It may ring for a fire and prevent a conflagration. In short, a church bell is a possession and a treasure to the whole community in the midst of which it is place.[2]

That text is an advertisement, the message of which is "buy a bell from us." However, advertising only works when it appeals to a mindset already predisposed to value what is being sold. A comment by H. B. Walters in his 1908 book *"Church Bells"* gives us a glimpse into what those who bought bells and shipped them to China might have been thinking:

Those to whom such things are a concern have begun to realize that a bell is a vehicle of history, and that, therefore, its history should be

---

2. "Value of Church Bells," *brosamerbells.com.* Accessed September 18, 2016.

7

duly recorded and preserved. But what is of far more importance, they have also learned to look upon it as an instrument destined for God's service—as one of the "Ornaments of the Church"—and therefore just as deserving of honor as any other furniture of God's house.[3]

The bells that I found are just that—vehicles of history. They have deepened my understanding of the history of the church in China, which is ultimately the story of God's sustaining grace. A closer look at the timelines of the churches—when they were built; when they were destroyed; when they were rebuilt; when they were confiscated; and when they were returned—gives us snapshots of important historical events in China. The dates are not random. They have meaning, for they are all tied directly to the major social, economic, and political events of the day.

After I found that first bell in Yibin, I called my friend Amy in Beijing to tell her what we had seen. "If there is one surviving bell here in Yibin," I told her, "there are hundreds of bells all over the country. And each has a story. I want to discover those stories."

This book is a collection of stories of the bells that I found before moving back to the United States. Each is comprised of three intertwined stories. One is a story of discovering the bells themselves, not always an easy task. Imagine a foreigner showing up at a church in China and saying "Hello. I would like to climb up into your steeple." Another is the story of the particular church and bell. Where did it come from, and how did it survive China's tumultuous years? The third story is the most important, yet perhaps the least obvious: namely the story of God's faithfulness and sustaining grace to the church in China.

---

3. H.B. Walters, "Church Bells," (1908): Kindle edition location 888.

Lu Jiao Yuan Christian Church
Yibin, Sichuan Province

Ben crawled along the dusty cement beam near where the giant bell was hanging in the steeple, shining his flashlight on it and reading out the letters engraved on the side. Down below in the swiftly fading light, Noël and I stood ready to capture it all. She had her audio recording app open on her phone, and I had my pen and notebook ready.

He read out the letters, one by one: "B. U. C. K. E. Y. E."

Noël and I looked at each other in bewilderment. "Buckeye?"

He continued reading what was written on the old bell: "Buckeye Bell Foundry, Cincinnati. First Baptist Church Coffeyville, Kansas. Presented by W. S. Upham, 1886. Praise Ye the Lord."

We were stunned. Here we were, face-to-face with a bell cast in Ohio for a church in Kansas, hanging in a steeple in western China.

My mind swirled as I thought about the turmoil the bell had witnessed during its century in China: the revolution in 1911 that toppled the Qing Dynasty and brought an end to two thousand years of dynastic rule; the Warlord era, when China effectively broke up into regional fiefdoms run by local warlords; the Japanese invasion and occupation; the Civil War between the Nationalists and Communists; "Liberation," when the Communist Party proclaimed the establishment of the "People's Republic of China" and began

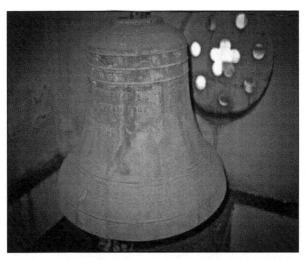

Close-up of the bell in the Lu Jiao Yuan Church

the fundamental transformation of an ancient nation; and the slow turn from Chairman Mao's China into the China of today.

The first thirty years of the People's Republic of China saw violent political campaigns as the Communist Party sought to bring all of life in China under its control. This included, but was not limited to, religious life. The government initially adopted a tolerant attitude towards Christianity and the remaining foreign missionaries working there. That tolerance ran out in the early 1950's, helped along by the outbreak of hostilities on the Korean peninsula. The remaining foreign missionaries were expelled.

Seeking to consolidate its power over every aspect of life in China, the Communist Party set about bringing the religious sphere under its control. To bring Christianity to heel, it launched the

Lu Jiao Yuan Christian Church

Church Unification Campaign in 1952. Foreign denominations were abolished and churches were forced to join a non-denominational political organization called the Three-Self Patriotic Movement Committee (TSPM), a group whose mission was to ensure the loyalty of the Protestant Church to the new regime. Where a city had three or four churches, perhaps one Presbyterian, one Anglican, one Baptist, and one Lutheran, three were closed and all Christians forced to attend one. Pastors who refused to join this newly formed national church were imprisoned. Many believers who were unsatisfied with this turn of events formed illegal congregations outside of the system. This was the genesis of the house church movement, which continues to this day and has grown to include perhaps forty million people.

Our research trip into the life of Esther Nelson had brought us to Yibin, a remote city of five million people in Sichuan, most famous in China for its potent rice wine.

We were being shepherded around Sichuan by our intrepid guide and friend Ben, a Sichuan native who had been introduced to me by another friend. That's how things are done in China; friends introduce you to friends who can help. He had graciously cleared his schedule for a week to help us, and had picked us up at the train station at Emei Mountain to drive us to Yibin, Ya'an, and back to Chengdu, where he lived. He had even brought along his 85-year-old father. Instead of the steamers and sedan chairs that Esther had used, we were now road-tripping Sichuan in a Volvo.

In our research prior to the visit, we had come to the conclusion that the Lu Jiao Yuan Christian Church in Yibin was most likely the "descendent church" of the one started by the American Baptist Missionaries in the early 1900's. Before our arrival, Ben had contacted Pastor Zhao to arrange a visit. Like every pastor I have ever met in China, he was an extremely busy man; nevertheless, he graciously invited us to visit him at the church. On a late Thursday afternoon, after a drive across the mountains of central Sichuan,

11

we met him in his office to learn what we could about the history of his church.

The Lu Jiao Yuan Christian Church was founded in 1896 by missionaries from the American Baptist Foreign Mission Society (ABFMS), and served as the base of operations for their work in Yibin, then called Xufu, and southern Sichuan. After the missionaries were expelled in the 1950's, the church came under the supervision of the Three Self Patriotic Committee Movement (TSPM). It remained open until the 1960's when Chairman Mao, fearing that he was losing his grip on power within the Chinese Communist Party, launched his most daring and brutal political campaign, the Great Proletarian Cultural Revolution.

The ten years of the Cultural Revolution were a time of economic, social, and political chaos. The economy ground to a halt as everyone went out to make revolution. The Party called for the overthrow of all vestiges of ancient Chinese culture, destroying thousands of temples and historical sites all over the country. Neighbor was turned against neighbor and family member against family member. Even Communist Party members were not spared as Mao persecuted and killed officials whom he suspected of not being loyal.

It was during this time that Christianity came under more direct assault. As everything in Chinese life became more political, Christianity was increasingly viewed as being a foreign religion and Christians as enemies and potential traitors. Anything that was considered foreign was to be abolished or destroyed. It was during this time that the Party decided it wanted to rid society of religion altogether, forcing the closure of all religious venues. Temples, mosques, and churches were taken over by local Party governments and turned into schools, factories, and warehouses.

The bells were silent.

The death of Chairman Mao in 1976 brought an end to the Cultural Revolution. Mao's successor, Deng Xiaoping launched a campaign to modernize the country and begin opening it to the outside world. Eventually China began to engage diplomatically on the world stage, and internally the Party began a gradual turn away from dogmatic Marxism. It instituted free-market economic reforms and began to loosen its grip on the lives of Chinese citizens. This easing included the relaxation of its anti-religious policies. The ban on religious activities was lifted. All across the country church buildings were returned to their congregations and pastors were released from prison. As pastors and parishioners returned to their buildings, they found that many of the church artifacts had been removed or destroyed—pews, pulpits, stained glass windows, and bells. The arduous process of restoring their places of worship began.

As religious policies continued to relax over the coming decades, many more churches reopened. By the late 1990's some of the lost bells had made their way home, each with a story to tell. Many of them would no longer be silent .

The church was re-opened in the 1980's, and the elderly pastor released from jail. In 1998 the old building was torn down to make way for the current structure, which was completed and opened in 2000. Where the old church building could only seat three hundred to four hundred people, this one seats over a thousand.

[4]After a couple of hours of drinking tea and poring over old documents, piecing together the story of the church and finding points of connection to our research, the pastor asked us if we could help him with something.

"There's an old bell in our steeple," he said. "It has English writing

---

4. By 1958, Chairman Mao was growing impatient with the pace of industrialization and modernization. To jump-start the process he launched the Great Leap Forward, an audacious campaign that promised to catapult China past Great Britain in terms of modernization within twenty years. He urged everyone to melt down iron in their homes for use in steelmaking, and ordered peasants in the countryside to build "backyard furnaces" to produce steel. Unfortunately, when peasants are making steel, they are not growing food. The resulting famine led to the deaths of tens of millions of people.

on it, but we can't read it. Perhaps you can translate it for us." Of course we were eager to see this bell with English writing on it.

The sun was setting as we made our way through the church towards the steeple. At the top of the stairs we stepped outside onto a lovely rooftop courtyard, which afforded us a great view of the neighborhood that included a few old structures that previously housed the Baptist school and missionary residences. From there we climbed a rickety spiral staircase up into the steeple.

As we entered the steeple, we immediately spotted the bell hanging from the ceiling; unfortunately, it was too high for us to get a good look at. There was a cement beam stretching across the inside of the steeple just beside the bell, so we reasoned that if we could get on that beam we could get a good look at the bell and read the inscription.

Pastor Zhao fetched a ladder but refused to let Noël or me climb up there. He was happy that we were there, but no way was he going to risk having two injured foreign women on his hands! Ben, who is younger and much more athletic, grabbed his flashlight and scampered up to get a good look at the inscription. It was from this perch, high up in the steeple, that he read the inscription to us.

From the conversations we had with the pastor that night and subsequent research, I managed to link together bits and pieces of the bell's story.

In the mid 1800's a man named W. S. Upham moved from San Francisco to Coffeyville, Kansas, where he became a wealthy merchant who was generous in his giving to his church, the First Baptist Church. Based on the inscription, we can assume that he was the one who commissioned and paid for the casting of the bell.

It's not surprising that he would have chosen the Buckeye Bell Foundry to make the bell, since at that time it was one of the premier foundries in the United States. Founded in 1837 by George Coffin, the Buckeye Bell Foundry was known for its ornate bells. In 1865 one of Coffin's apprentices, a Mr. Vanduzen, purchased the foundry and renamed it after himself. The foundry remained operational until the 1950's. From 1909 to 1928 the president of the company was Samuel P. Bush, grandfather to President G. H. W. Bush and great-grandfather to President G. W. Bush.[5]

A short article published by the Vanduzen Bell Company in the 1920's boasts of the popularity of their bells:

The Lu Jiao Yuan Christian Church in Yibin, Sichuan.

We have furnished over 60,000 bells used in churches, schools, and public buildings. We have bells in some of the most remote corners of the world, in Europe, Asia, Australia, South America, Mexico,

5. "A History of Columbus Castings," *ColumbusCastings.com*, accessed September 18, 2016, http://www.columbuscastings.com/history.html.

and a great number in Canada, and in nearly every city, town, and hamlet in the United States.[6]

I wonder if they knew then that one of their earliest bells was hanging in a church in a remote corner of war-torn China. It is likely that the bell hung in the tower of the First Baptist Church in Coffeyville, Kansas until 1907, the year that congregation built a new sanctuary. At this point I can imagine a committee meeting at the church where one of the agenda items was a discussion of what to do with the old church bell. Should it be melted down? Should it be placed in the new church building? Should it be donated to another church? Then someone, perhaps Mr. Upham himself, suggests donating the bell to the Mission Board so they can send it to China to be used in a church built there.

We don't know how the decision was made or who made it, but around 1907, some person or persons took the initiative to ship a quarter-ton bell from a small town in Kansas to a small city in Sichuan. It would have been an arduous journey: by train to the west coast; by ship across the Pacific Ocean; by boat up the Yangtze River to Chongqing; then another boat up the Min River to Yibin. The journey would have taken perhaps six months to a year.

Pastor Zhao told us that the bell hung in the church until the Cultural Revolution in the 1960's, when the local authorities closed the church and demolished the bell tower. The bell was taken to a local factory.

The church remained closed until the mid-1980's. Shortly afterwards, the pastor at the time got word from someone at the local Catholic Church that their old bell was in a nearby factory. He asked the local Religious Affairs Bureau to help them secure the return of their bell. In 1993 the factory finally agreed to return the bell, but only after paying a *"baoguan fei"* (protection fee), which

---

6. "Just a Little Bell History," *BrosamerBells.com*, accessed September 18, 2016, http://www.brosamersbells.com/1histpix/vdbellhist.gif.

the church of course was happy to do. In this case, most likely the *"baoguan fei"* was a face-saving way for the factory to secure some cash in exchange for handing over the bell. The bell was formally returned to the church on August 19, 1993. Pastor Zhao, who was a seminary student at the time, was home for summer break and went with the old pastor to retrieve it.

When the new church building was constructed in 2000 they made sure it had a steeple to house the bell, which is now rung every Sunday morning to mark the beginning of worship.

In 1993 Astrid Peterson, a 91-year-old former missionary to Yibin who would have worked and worshipped in this church, travelled back to China with Mildred Lovegren, another former missionary. When she arrived in Yibin she was thrilled, not just that the church was open again, but that they had gotten their bell back. Following her visit, the Three-Self Church magazine *Tianfeng* published a story about the bell and Astrid's visit to the church. A translation of that article appears in the book *"Millie's China"* by Edie Lambert:

> *In Yibin, Sichuan, there was a big copper bell in the Yibin Christian Church. It was made in 1860 in Cincinnati, Ohio. The workmanship is very fine. It weighed 551 pounds. The inscription on the bell explains that it was given by the Baptist Church in Coffeeville, Kansas, and presented by their pastor Rev. W. S. Upham. [inaccuracies in translation]*
>
> *When the bell was rung, the sound was clear and stern, so the whole city was able to hear it. Unfortunately, during the Cultural Revolution the bell was taken down and moved to a machine factory in the southern part of Yibin (the church had been closed).*
>
> *When the church was reopened, they started long negotiations about their bell. With the help of the Religious Affairs Department, the church got their bell back on August 19, 1993. The church and the Religious Affairs Department held a formal celebration on that*

broadcast station of Yibin announced the news to the whole city.
Thanks was given to the government, particularly to the Religious
Affairs Department that assisted in the return of the bell. On
August 25, 1993 Miss Astrid Peterson, an American missionary,
came back to visit the church in Yibin. When she saw the bell, she
was exceedingly happy and pictures were taken of her and the bell.[7]

After descending the stairs from the steeple, we paused on the
rooftop for a while to watch as nightfall enveloped the bustling city.
I was, of course, still thinking about the bell. How had it endured?

After we were back inside the sanctuary I asked Pastor Zhao,
"How did this bell survive the Great Leap Forward, when every
scrap of metal was melted down?"

"They tried to destroy it," he said, "but they couldn't; it was too
strong."

Just like the church in China, I thought. They tried to destroy
it, but it was too strong. It was at that moment the bell became a
symbol for me of God's faithfulness to the Church in China.

---

7. Edie Lambert, *Millie's China*, (USA: Promist Publishing Company, 1998), 188–189.

Xuanwumen Catholic Church
Beijing

The Xuanwumen neighborhood to the west of Tiananmen Square in Beijing consists primarily of central government buildings and residence complexes for government workers. They are imposing neo-Stalinist structures that seem to declare, "I am in charge and I do not approve of aesthetics." In the middle of it all, at one of the busiest intersections in the city, stands the Cathedral of the Immaculate Conception, also known as *Nan Tang* (South Church). Locally it is mostly referred to as Xuanwumen Catholic Church. Even though the building only dates to 1904, there has been a Catholic church of some type on this site since 1605, making this the oldest church in Beijing. It is the seat of the Beijing Diocese, which means that there is an archbishop in residence. His name is Joseph Li Shan, and he has the distinction of being one of the few Catholic bishops in China who is recognized by both the Vatican and the Chinese government.

The church was founded by Matteo Ricci, an Italian Jesuit who arrived in Beijing in 1601, after having lived in Zhaoqing, Shaozhou, Nanchang and Nanjing, all cities in southern China. He was the first foreigner to be given permission to live in the city. This was a big deal because at the time foreigners were forbidden. If one were to be discovered in the city, he, and anyone who helped him, would be executed. Emperor Wanli, however, was so impressed by Ricci's knowledge of the Confucian classics that he not only allowed him

Xuanwumen Catholic Church in Beijing

to take up residence in the city, he granted Ricci a piece of land to the west of the Forbidden City, near where the church stands today. Ricci promptly built a small chapel.

He died in Beijing in 1610 and was buried in a cemetery that the emperor had set aside for Catholic missionaries. Red Guards destroyed the cemetery during the Cultural Revolution; however, some of the commemorative stones survived. Today they are classified as "protected relics" by the Antiquities Bureau and are kept on the grounds of the Communist Party Administration School in the western part of Beijing. I have always enjoyed the irony of the Communist Party being in charge of protecting the graves of the first missionaries to the city.

Xuanwumen Catholic Church

Catholicism is one of the five recognized, legal religions in China, the others being Buddhism, Taoism, Islam, and Protestant Christianity. When I first went to China, I remember being asked what I thought at the time was a very strange question: "What is the difference between Christian and Catholic?" The question itself made no sense to me; it was like asking, "What is the difference between a Volkswagen and a car?"

The confusion was understandable in the 1980's because many Chinese at that time had almost no knowledge of religion, let alone western religions. Truth be told, they had no idea what either of those terms, Catholic or Christian, meant. It wasn't until I studied Chinese that I came to realize that the oddness of the question was rooted in linguistics. Catholicism is Christianity, but in the Chinese language it has a completely different name.

In English we distinguish between different strands of Christianity: Catholic, Protestant, and Orthodox. But in the Chinese language only one of those strands gets translated as "religion of Christ," "Christianity."

The Chinese word for Catholicism is *Tian Zhu Jiao* (天主教), "Religion of the Lord of Heaven." Matteo Ricci wrote a book called "The True Meaning of the Lord of Heaven," in which he attempted to link the God of the Bible with the traditional religious notion of a supreme being, which was referred to as Heaven. It thus became known as the Religion of the Lord of Heaven, *Tian Zhu Jiao*.

When Protestantism came to China it was necessary to distinguish it from Catholicism, As a result it was translated as *Jidu Jiao* (基督教), "Religion of Christ." This then gets translated back into English as "Christianity." Hence the odd question about the difference between Catholicism and Christianity.

The Xuanwumen Catholic Church is affiliated with the Chinese Patriotic Catholic Association, or the officially recognized Catholic Church. Similar to the Three-Self Patriotic Movement Committee for the Protestant churches, its aim is to ensure the loyalty of the Church to the government. Today the Catholic Church in China does not refer to itself as the Roman Catholic Church because the government prohibits it from swearing allegiance to the Pope, who is a political monarch of the Vatican as well as the spiritual head of the Church. The Chinese government simply will not let a foreigner be the spiritual leader of Chinese believers, nor will it tolerate Chinese swearing allegiance to a foreign power.

Despite the pressures, there are numerous Catholic Churches all over the country serving Chinese believers who are trying to practice their faith as best they can. Xuanwumen Church is one of those churches.

In 1690 a fellow Jesuit named Johann Adam Schall von Bell began building a new church on the site. Like Ricci before him, von Bell had impressed the Emperor Kangxi, and had even become his friend. Perhaps because of this friendship the emperor had a tolerant attitude toward von Bell's religion, and often visited and inscribed steles (stone tablets) to be placed in the church courtyard.

The 18th century was a difficult one for the church. A new European-style structure was built in 1703, but was destroyed in an earthquake in 1720. The diocese built a new one, but it too was damaged in an earthquake in 1730. After being repaired, it was damaged by fire in 1775.

By 1838 the relationship between the Church and the new monarch, Emperor Daoguang, had deteriorated to the point where he restricted all Catholic activity in the city and confiscated the building and the land. It remained closed until 1860, when, as a result of its defeat in the Second Opium War, China was forced to sign a treaty that required the opening of China's interior to foreigners, including missionaries.[8]

In the summer of 1900, the Boxers laid siege to the city of

8. "Catholic Churches in Beijing," *China Zentrum*, accessed September 18, 2016. http://china-zentrum.de/Churches-in-China.354.0.html?&L=1.

Beijing, destroying all of the Catholic and Protestant churches and massacring thousands of Chinese Christians who had sought shelter in the church compounds. The current church building, an imposing and gorgeous Italian Baroque structure, was built in 1904.

Brother Liu, the husband of a dear friend of mine, had become

One of the bells in the Xuanwumen Catholic Church

fascinated with these bell stories, and so had offered to serve as our bell-hunting driver. A local Beijing entrepreneur, he was very well connected, even within church circles. He was able to get us into the church because he knew one of the priests, which meant that when we showed up on a sunny Saturday afternoon, we were ushered right in.

Like most churches in China, this one sits inside a walled

courtyard that keeps the noise of the city at bay. Within the courtyard there are smaller buildings that house offices and living quarters of some church staff, including a sweet English-speaking nun named Sister Theresa. There is also a statute of Matteo Ricci and two carved steles, one presented by Emperor Shunzhi and the other by Emperor Qianlong.

The priest led us up into the baroque-style octagonal tower that was located above the altar instead of above the main entrance. There we found two identical bells, hung at differing heights. On the bell that was low enough for us to see, there was a cross and an inscription that read "Eduard Biron Fonfeur, Paris." There was no date, but it is easy to presume that it was cast and hung in 1904 when the church was rebuilt following the Boxer Rebellion.

As always, we were faced with the question of how the bells had been left unharmed. When the church was closed during the Cultural Revolution it was taken over by a nearby school.

How did the bells survive? Perhaps no one remembered that they were up there. Or perhaps someone tried to destroy them, but they were too strong. The bells are no longer silent, however; they are rung each Sunday morning to mark the beginning of Mass.

Xizhimen Catholic Church
Beijing

In late September of 2012, Beijing had taken on the feel of a city under siege as it was gearing up for the 18th Communist Party Congress scheduled for October. This was the big one; the mother lode of Communist Party meetings, held every five years to determine the leadership of the Party for the coming five years. The Congress that year was particularly important because the Party was set to announce an entirely new leadership line-up—the names of seven men who would form the Standing Committee of the Politburo of the Chinese Communist Party. It would introduce to the nation and the world the men who would rule China for the next ten years. Even though it was widely known who these men would be, the Party was still jittery and demanding that the event go off without a hitch.

Nothing was being left to chance. Everyone was mobilized to maintain stability and social order. Neighborhood grannies were deputized to keep an eye on the comings and goings in the *hutongs*, the small alleyways that make up the old city. Anyone who had a job that kept them out and about was sporting a red armband, identifying that they were "on patrol." This included security guards, street peddlers, supermarket checkout clerks, and waitresses.

No institution was spared involvement in making sure the city remained calm and secure, not even the churches. Pastors in Prot-

Xizhimen Catholic Church in Beijing

estant and Catholic churches were told to deputize their members for special duties to make sure the churches were safe and would not become platforms for anti-Party activities.

Everyone in the city was on edge because no one knew when an inspection team from the Communist Party would swoop in to check on things.

It was in this environment that Brother Liu drove Amy, Jessie, and me to a small Catholic church tucked away on a narrow street to the east of the giant Xizhimen highway interchange.

Amy, my friend and colleague, had caught my "bell fever" right from the beginning, when I had called her excitedly from Yibin to tell her about finding that first bell. Over our fifteen years of working together in China, we had already logged more adventures than we could count; so adding bell hunting to the mix seemed perfectly natural. Jessie, a local university student whom I had gotten to know at one of the local Protestant churches, joined our team that day as the translator.

Locally the church is known as either the Xizhimen Catholic Church or *Xi Tang* (West Church), but its official name is the Church of Our Lady of Mt. Carmel. It was founded in 1723 by an Italian Lazarist missionary named Teolorica Pedrini.

Pedrini arrived in 1711 with a fellow Lazarist Mattao Ripa; they have the distinction of being the first two non-Jesuits to work in Beijing. In addition to being a priest and missionary, Pedrini was an accomplished musician. In fact, he had been invited to Beijing by Emperor Kangxi to introduce western music to the Qing Court and to teach music to his sons, a prestigious appointment.

Imperial China was generally not welcoming to foreigners, and most foreign contact was limited to traders, who were allowed into Canton (Guangzhou) every year for trade purposes. It wasn't until the 1500's that the first foreigner, a Jesuit missionary, was allowed to reside in Beijing. In the case of both the Jesuits and the Lazarists, the emperor deemed that their knowledge and skills were useful to him, and thus he appointed them to court positions.

Pedrini was also a major figure in what has come to be known as the Rites Controversy that raged within the Catholic missions community in the 18th century. This controversy centered on the question of whether Christian converts should be allowed to continue practicing Confucian rites and rituals following their conversion. The Jesuits argued that the rites were not really religious practices, but cultural; therefore converts should be allowed to continue practicing them. The other orders, including the Dominicans and the Lazarists, considered the rites to be religious practices; therefore Christian converts must give them up. The dispute was not always a civil one. Pedrini was actually imprisoned by the Jesuits in Beijing at one point. Pope Clement XI eventually settled the matter in 1715, taking the position that the Catholic converts must give up practicing the Confucian rites.

Not surprisingly, this and subsequent decrees governing the lives of Chinese Catholics infuriated the emperor. In 1723, the very year that the church was built, he banned Catholicism.

The church was destroyed in 1811, rebuilt in 1867, and destroyed again in 1900 during the Boxer Rebellion. It was closed from 1958 to 1994, and during that time the building housed variously a button factory, a fan factory, and a pharmaceutical warehouse. The bell tower was also destroyed during the Cultural Revolution, and was not rebuilt until 2007.

Because of our fear of being turned down, we had not called ahead to arrange our visit; it's harder to say no to people standing at the gate than at the other end of a phone line. A kind lay worker greeted us at the gate and, after Brother Liu introduced us and told him what we were researching, invited us into the church compound. He seemed eager to tell us the story of his church. As he was showing us around the church compound, he told us that he was a member of the Manchu minority and was a descendant of a clan of Manchus who had been severely persecuted in the 1700's because they had converted to Christianity.

At that time, most of the converts to Christianity were Han. The Qing rulers were Manchu people from the northeast, and despite the fact that the emperor was tolerant of mission work conducted by the Catholics, his tolerance only extended to their work among the Han. He did not approve of members of his own ethnic group converting. By the early 1700's, however, there were a few Manchu converts.

In his book *"A New History of Christianity in China"* Daniel Bays writes about this group of Manchu converts during the Qing Dynasty:

The bell in the Xizhimen Catholic Church in Beijing

After the handover of power to the new Qing regime, and the Jesuits' success in maintaining residence in Beijing, the congregation of believers continued to grow. By 1700 it included a small but increasing number of ethnic Manchus. Several of these were from the Sunu family. Sunu was a cousin of the Yongzheng Emperor, who reigned 1723-1735. After Yongzheng's prohibition of Christianity in 1723, he punished the Christians in Sunu's clan over the next few years and Manchu converts seem to have disappeared, except for perhaps a handful. Despite the hostile atmosphere, a small number of converts, 2,000 or so, continued to exist in Beijing through most of the 18th century.[9]

After the fall of the Qing Dynasty in 1911, many Manchu remained in Beijing, and now, here we were, talking with a man who was a descendant of the Sunu clan—still believing, still serving. Today there are more than ten million Manchus in China, and although their cultural traditions and language have largely died out, they are still classified as one of China's fifty-five ethnic minority groups.

Before he could take us up to see the church bells, our guide's cell phone rang: it was someone calling from the church office alerting him that a security inspection team was on its way to the church! The foreigners had to leave NOW! We thanked him profusely and rushed back to the car, hoping to make our getaway before the inspection team arrived. The last thing the church leaders need to do was explain the presence of foreigners poking around.

The following spring we returned to the church, and although the Manchu caretaker wasn't there, we were able to climb into the steeple to see their bells. The original bells had long since disappeared and the ones hanging now were cast in 2007 to commemorate the rebuilding of the steeple and reopening of the church following extensive renovations.

The bells may be new, but the message proclaimed each week as they are rung is not, namely "the old, old story of Jesus and his love."[10]

---

9. Daniel Bays, *A New History of Christianity in China*, (USA: John Wiley & Sons, 2011). 26.
10. Kate Hankey, "Tell Me the Old, Old Story," *Hymnary.org*, accessed September 18, 2016, http://www.hymnary.org/text/tell_me_the_old_old_story_of_unseen_things_above.

A Linguistic Hurdle

In the process of gathering these bell stories, I kept getting tripped up by a linguistic hurdle, namely the correct translation of the world "bell."

Chinese is first and foremost a written language, with a writing system that uses characters. Each character depicts a meaning, not a sound as a letter in an alphabet does. There are an estimated total of 50,000 characters; however, most are not commonly used. An educated person is said to have mastery of approximately 8,000, and there are only 2,000 to 3,000 in everyday use.

When I was studying Chinese, I was told that I would be able to read a Chinese newspaper when I had learned 2,000 characters. Unfortunately, when I hit that mark and opened up a newspaper, it seemed to me as if I had learned the wrong 2,000!

In spoken Chinese, there are only 404 phonetic words used to pronounce those 50,000 characters. What I mean by phonetic word is a specific way that the character is pronounced. The character for bell is 钟. It is pronounced *zhong*, so that would be the phonetic word. The spelling of that word is based on a system called Pinyin, which is a phonetic transcription of how the word is pronounced. To make things even more complicated, different phonetic words are said with different tones: high-flat, rising, dipping, or falling. In this case, *zhong* is said using the high-flat, or first tone.

To top it off, because there are a limited number of characters available to convey meaning, each character is called upon to convey multiple meanings.

This means that knowing the context is important.

If someone asks verbally "What does *zhong* mean?" there's really no easy way to answer. Which *zhong*? The *zhong* said with a rising tone or a falling tone? And once that is established, which character is it? There are twenty-four different characters that are pronounced *zhong*. Many of the characters have multiple meanings, ranging from seed to important to goblet to grasshopper.

As I mentioned earlier, the Chinese word for bell is *zhong* (钟). Unfortunately that character is also the word for "clock." This means that when I began to ask someone about a bell or bells, upon simply hearing me say the word, the listener, although probably quite certain that I was not asking about a seed or a grasshopper, they had no way of knowing whether I was talking about a bell or a clock. This was especially tricky in the city of Qingdao, where the tower of the church houses both a bell and a clock. Furthermore, the bell and clock are one mechanical instrument!

To let the person I was talking to know that I was looking for a bell and not a clock, in typically silly foreigner fashion I simply mimicked the sound of a bell—*gong, gong*—and waved my hands as though I were hitting a bell. Unfortunately I found out later that I wasn't even doing that correctly, because the way to indicate the sound of a bell in Chinese is actually *hong, hong*. Fortunately, Chinese are generally good at figuring out what foreigners are trying to say, so they usually got my meaning.

I finally asked a friend how to disentangle this linguistic mess and was told that I should say *dazhong* (大钟) when referring to a bell. The literal meaning of this term is "big bell" and it is the most common word used to distinguish a bell from a clock. In hindsight, I should have known this because for years I worked in an office in the Beijing neighborhood of *Da Zhong Si* (大钟寺), which means Big Bell Temple.

There are other words for bell in Chinese as well. One is *duo* (铎), but that wasn't an option because it specifically refers to ancient bell used in Buddhist and Taoist temples. The other word is *yong* (镛), which refers to a large bell used as a musical instrument.

There were many hurdles along the way, mental and physical, but since I am endlessly curious and not easily thwarted, the search for the Chinese church bells continued.

A traditional Chinese bell used in a Buddhist temple

Xikai Catholic Church
Tianjin, China

Even though it happened on numerous occasions I was still a little surprised when we showed up at a church gate and were given entrance to see the priest or pastor. Because Chinese culture is an "insider-outsider" culture, walls, gates, and gatekeepers have pride of place in society. They not only delineate what is inside from what is outside, they also protect what is inside from what is outside.

We told the gatekeeper who we were and what our mission was; he had said to wait and headed into the compound. "Hey Father," he probably said, "There are three foreigners at the gate wanting to talk to you. Should I just send them away?" In this case, Father Zhang, perhaps out of curiosity, had said we could enter; thus we found ourselves in the office of the priest of Xikai Catholic Church, Tianjin's largest Catholic Church.

"Why are you so interested in bells?" Father Zhang asked us. "There's nothing especially interesting about bells."

Joining me on this trip were Amy; Megan, an American friend living in Tianjin; and Spring, a Chinese friend from Beijing. Even though my Chinese is fluent enough for everyday conversations, whenever possible I wanted to have a Chinese translator with me to help with the details that I was likely to miss. Until that point I had let Spring, a bubbly and outgoing "go-getter," do all the talking,

Xikai Catholic Church in Tianjin

explaining to him that these crazy foreigners from Beijing were doing research on old church bells. This, however, was a question I wanted to answer myself.

I told him about finding the old bell in Yibin and other cities and that each surviving bell in China has a story, and that story is the story of God's love for the church in China.

His countenance immediately changed and I moved from being simply a foreigner who was a pest to a foreigner who was to be helped, and perhaps even liked. As we kept talking, he started rummaging through a notebook on his desk, looking for something.

He told us that there were two old bells in the tower, one bronze and one steel, which dated back to the early 1900's. Unfortunately, his refusal to allow us to go up and see them was resolute. "It's not safe," he said over and over in response to our pleadings. I'm sure he was running through his mind a long list of ills that would befall him should a foreigner be injured climbing around in the steeples of his church; it just wasn't worth the risk.

The history of Tianjin is similar to that of Shanghai, in that from the mid-1880's until the mid-1900's it was divided into different foreign "concessions," areas of the city where foreign powers maintained sovereignty. This came about over time as the result of treaties and demands put upon the decrepit and nearly bankrupt Qing Dynasty government by the foreign powers, often in response to some anti-foreign incident.

The concessions belonged to the United States, England, Italy, France, Japan, Russia, Belgium, and Germany, and each of them had their own unique "flavor." In the concession areas, Chinese law did not apply; the law of the occupier did. Herbert Hoover, who would later become the 31st President of the United States, lived in the American section during the Boxer Rebellion in 1900 as a representative of an American mining company.[11] Another famous resident was Eric Liddell, the Christian Olympic runner made famous in the movie "Chariots of Fire." He lived there prior to the Japanese occupation, at which time he and most of the other foreign residents of the city were transferred to a prison camp in Shandong Province.[12]

Construction of Xikai Church was completed in 1916 using bricks imported from France. Once consecrated it served as the cathedral for the Diocese of Tianjin. It was forced to close during the Cultural Revolution, and in April 1966 Red Guards destroyed the crosses on top of the towers. In 1976 the Tangshan earthquake heavily damaged the towers themselves. They were not rebuilt until

---

11. "Years of Adventure, " *Herbert Hoover Presidential Library and Museum*, accessed September 18, 2016, http://hoover.archives.gov/exhibits/Hooverstory/gallery01/.
12. "A Short Biography of Eric H. Liddell (1902-1945)," *The Eric Liddell Centre*, accessed September 1, 2016, http://www.ericliddell.org/ericliddell/biography.

1980, when the government began to relax its policies towards religion.

"We do have a small bell I can let you see," the priest said, as he found the small, weathered piece of paper he had been searching for. He handed it to us and said, "Take a picture of this." It was a hand-written note that said "I found this bell at Linqing, Shandong Province in 1999 when I went there for shopping. Now I want to donate it to the church for free." It was signed and dated December 14, 2009.

"Would you like to see *this* bell?" Father Zhang asked us.

Trying to hide our disappointment at not being able to see the bells in the tower, but excitedly curious about this Chinese bell, we replied, "Of course!"

Father Zhang, his assistant in tow, took us to a shed behind the church building where we found an old iron bell under a table. It was too heavy to move out from under the table so we had to content ourselves with crawling around underneath the rickety table to get some photos. It was quite a change from climbing around in steeples!

What distinguished this bell from the others we had found was that it had been cast in China and looked more like a traditional Chinese-shaped bell. Long before cathedral bells were being cast in the west, Chinese were already using them as musical instruments and for official court functions. The earliest ones that have been discovered date back to around 2000 B.C. Like the bells that were developed later in the west, *zhong* often had inscriptions on them to commemorate important events. Later these bells came to feature prominently in Buddhist and Taoist ceremonies.

There are two main differences between western bells and *zhong*. The first is shape. Where western bells almost always have a wider base, *zhong* are more cylindrical in shape; the opening at the bottom is nearly the same diameter as the top. The second difference is in how they are struck. Western bells have internal clappers that produce a sound when they strike the inside wall of the bell.

Zhong do not have internal clappers; instead they are struck with a wooden mallet or beam from the outside. This gives it a much lower-pitched and more resonant sound.

The dusty bell we found underneath the table seemed to be

The old bell at Xikai Catholic Church

a blend of western and Chinese bell styles. The top was straight, much as a traditional *zhong* would be. However, the bottom had a slight lip, as if the caster were trying to make it look like other bells he had perhaps seen in a church. There were two holes carved into the sides of the bell at the top, most likely so a pole could be inserted and used to carry or suspend the bell.

We were able to make out some of the inscription:

天主将生 一千五百三年
(The Lord of Heaven Has Come to Earth 1530)
武定府
(Wudingfu [the name of a town])

The rest of the text was illegible to us, no matter how hard we tried to decipher it.

天主降生 (Tian Zhu jiang sheng) is best translated as "The Lord of Heaven has come." It was possible the bell had been cast for an Advent celebration. We were most puzzled by the date inscribed on the bell –1530. What did that refer to? It is too late to be a reference to the birth of Jesus, and too early to be a reference to a specific Catholic Church in China.

Later we called the number on the piece of paper and talked with the recycler himself. He told us of finding the bell in a village in Shandong Province. As a child he remembered hearing church bells in his village, and so understood that they were important to a church. Even though he was not a believer, he took the bell to the church in Tianjin and donated it. The sacrificial generosity on the part of a poor recycler was not lost on us.

Another bell, another story of God's sustaining grace.

Ya'an Christian Church
Ya'an, Sichuan Province

The day after discovering the first bell in Yibin, Noël and I were in the city of Ya'an, home of the famous Bifengxia Panda Base, one of China's largest panda reserves. Unlike every other foreign visitor to the city, we had no plans to see the pandas. We were there to see if there was any legacy of the work of the American Baptist Foreign Mission Society (ABFMS), which had begun work there in 1894 with the opening of a hospital, school, and church. The irony was not lost on us that, despite the hardships of history, it is not the church that is endangered, but the pandas.

Ben had worked his usual magic, calling ahead and arranging for us to have dinner with the pastor of the Ya'an Christian Church. The pastor, a small and somewhat reserved woman in her forties, met us at a restaurant on the opposite side of the square in front of the church. Since we were still excited about the bell we had found the day before in Yibin, and because my dream of finding church bells all over China had already begun to grow, I asked her if the church had a bell. She told us that it did. At first she was reluctant to grant our request to see the bell, but once she heard the story of the Yibin bell, she agreed to let us see it.

We walked across the plaza to the church and made our way up to a second floor storage room beneath the steeple where the bell was mounted on a platform. It was a different type of bell than the one we had seen in Yibin, but it shared a common place of origin: Cincinnati, Ohio. The foundry, however, was different; this one had

The Ya'an Christian Church in Ya'an, Sichuan

been cast at the Blymer Foundry. We did not see any date inscribed on the bell.

The pastor didn't know the details of how the bell had survived the political campaigns, but said that it had been taken away by Red Guards in the 1960's and returned to the church in the 1990's. She suspected they had tried to destroy it, but were unable to. Even though the bell was brown, the inside was pockmarked black. Was it soot, perhaps evidence of attempted destruction?

I remembered the words of Pastor Zhao the day before: "They tried to destroy it, but it was too strong." Another bell, another symbol of God's faithfulness.

To help us with our research on Esther Nelson in Ya'an, Ben had contacted a local friend, Brother Xie, who was knowledgeable about the history, not only of the city, but the work of the missionaries there prior to 1949. My Chinese name is *Zhou Ning*, and since I am a teacher, the polite way to address me in China is *Zhou Laoshi*, Teacher Zhou. This is what Brother Xie called me.

As we gathered in our hotel lobby the next morning to begin our walkabout Brother Xie pulled me aside and told me that he knew two men, brothers, in town whose father had worked at the Baptist School in the 1940's and might remember Esther Nelson. He had tried to contact them, but they were not answering their cell phones. He apologized to me for not being able to introduce us to them.

After several hours of walking and getting the lay of the land, we found ourselves in a lovely park on a hill overlooking the city. We had come to the park to see an old structure—an abandoned building that had once been part of the Baptist School. Since it was Saturday afternoon, the park was filled with people sitting in clusters doing what Sichuan people do when they are not working: playing cards or mahjong and drinking tea, in this case outside to enjoy the warm spring sunshine.

As Noël and I were walking around the building taking pictures, Brother Xie came running up to us. "*Zhou Laoshi, Zhou Laoshi*. I have found them! The men I told you about this morning are here playing mahjong with their wives! Come with me!" In a city of five million people, most of whom were playing mahjong on a warm spring afternoon, we happened to find the two people in the city with whom we wanted to speak!

We followed Brother Xie as he led us to the four startled mahjong players, and before they knew what was going on, we dragged the two men away from their game so we could talk to them. Once they got over the initial shock of being interrupted by two foreigners, they seemed eager to help.

After talking with them for a while and hearing about their memories of the missionaries from their childhood, we showed them an old photo of the Baptist Church, with a bell clearly visible in the steeple. Their eyes lit up when they saw the photo. "We remember that bell," they said in unison.

They then proceeded to tell us that when they were young the church bell had functioned as the city clock. When it was rung at 7 a.m., people set off to work. When it was rung at noon, everyone knew it was time to go home, eat lunch, and have a rest. Since ancient times bells have been used to mark the passing of time, and that's just what this bell did.

I asked them how long after 1949 this had lasted. "Until 1958," they replied. Here was a church bell that was not silenced until a full eight years into Communist rule! I can't help but think of the comfort it must have been to believers during that time, as their space for religious practice began to shrink. Today the bell rings more rarely: when it sounds it marks the beginning of worship on Sundays.

Prior to the 1950's the city was called Yachow, and in 1918 Mr. Openshaw, a missionary there at the time, wrote a report on the building of the new church in the city. This is the one we had a photo of, and the one in which the bell we had seen originally hung. Describing the church, he wrote:

The new church is splendidly located in the very center of the city. The main auditorium will seat five hundred, and two hundred more can be seated in the Sunday-school and prayer-meeting room. A number of classrooms have been provided for in the main building, while guest rooms and larger classrooms will be housed in other buildings on the compound. With the completion of this building a valuable addition has been made to the working plant of the Yachow Station, and we trust that the more imposing building, centrally located, will make a stronger appeal to the whole community, and also enable us to do much more efficient work than has been possible heretofore.

Unusual difficulties have been experienced in the securing of materials and with the workmen. To my friend and colleague, Mr. Baily, belongs the credit of pushing the building through, and we will let him tell us sometime of his experiences.

The church will have two towers, in one of which the First Swedish Church of Minneapolis will place a large bell, in memory of dear Brother Axel Salquist, who laid down his life for the Master at Yachow. A little union Sunday School at New Brighton, Staten Island, with which the writer and his family had been connected for years, has very generously given $300.00 for an organ in the new church.[13]

According to the journal *Missions: A Baptist Monthly Magazine* (1911), Reverend Carl Axel Salquist died of yellow fever in Yachow in April of 1911. He had arrived in China in 1893, taking up his first post as an evangelist in Suifu (modern-day Yibin). In 1909 he moved to Yachow, where he directed the Bible Training School.[14]

Writing in the September 1937 mission report Openshaw described him as "a stalwart Swede from Minnesota."[15] He also writes about how he and Salquist met their wives: "A happy interlude came in this period

---

13. H.J. Openshaw, "The New Church at Yachow," *The Journal and Messenger: The Central National Baptist Newspaper, Volume 87,* (March 7, 1918): https://books. google.com/books?id=tMM7AQAAMAAJ&lpg=PR176&dq=church%20bell%20 yachow&pg=PR176#v=onepage&q=church%20bell%20yachow&f=false).
14. "Death of Rev. C.A. Salquist," *Missions: a Baptist Monthly Magazine,* Volume 2, (1911), 436–437. https://books.google.com/books?id=dpjNAAAAMAA-J&lpg=PA436&ots=TlXkn_wLAw&dq=axel%20salquist&pg=PA436#v=onep-age&q=436&f=false).
15. "Work of the West China Baptist Mission," *The West China Missionary News,* (September 1937): 13.

of service, the Winter of 1937, when Salquist and I made a record run to Shanghai to meet and marry two fine American girls—Misses Ericson and van Valkenburg."[16] We are left to wonder if the plans for the marriages had been pre-arranged and Miss Ericson and Miss Valken-

The bell in the Ya'an Church

burg were coming to China specifically to marry these two gentlemen or if, upon hearing that there were two single women on board a ship, the two bachelors hightailed it to Shanghai.

The First Swedish Church mentioned in Openshaw's article is, in fact, Bethlehem Baptist Church. It is my and Noël's home church, and the home church of Esther Nelson, the woman whose life we were researching. The church changed its name in the 1950's, but the records were clear. We now had a clear link between this church in Ya'an and our own church.

I was back in Minnesota when I made this discovery of the

_____

16. Ibid, .11.

connection, and remembered seeing an old bell in the entryway to Bethlehem. It had hung in the old sanctuary that had been torn down in 1990 to make way for the current one. Since the new sanctuary does not have a steeple, the old bell is now just tucked into a corner. Might there be a link between that bell and the one we had found in Ya'an? I wondered. I drove to the church to have a look.

The similarities, in terms of size, shape, and style are clear. Unfortunately, there is no inscription on the bell anywhere so it wasn't possible to confirm that the bells are twins. They do, however, share the same heart and message: that God is faithful to his church, both in China and in America.

Ukrainian Orthodox Church
Harbin, Heilongjiang

We spotted the bell in the tower of the small Orthodox Church in Harbin from the busy street. It was a Saturday, and Amy and I were walking around, enjoying a late autumn day in the capital of Heilongjiang Province. The building was locked up tight and looked as if it had been so for decades. I trained my telephoto lens on the bell, snapping away from a distance, figuring that was as close as we were likely to get.

I could not have been more wrong. By late Sunday morning, we, along with some new Russian and Chinese friends, were climbing into the tower to see the bell.

That we would find a bell in an historic Russian Orthodox Church in Harbin was not surprising. In fact, knowing of the city's Russian past, we had come specifically looking for Russian bells.

From the late 1800's until 1949 there was a sizeable population of Russians in the city. As the 19th century was winding down, the Qing Dynasty contracted with the Russians to build the rail line between Harbin and Beijing, thus bringing in the first wave of Russian settlers. During the Bolshevik Revolution the Russian population of the city swelled as ordinary people sought escape from war and the elites sought escape from the Bolsheviks. The Russian heritage of Harbin remains visible in scattered spots around the city, mostly in the form of old Orthodox churches.

The largest and most prominent church in the city, and the one we visited first, was St. Sophia's, formerly called the Cathedral of the Holy Wisdom of God. It sits proudly in a square in the heart of the city. No longer in use as a church, today it houses the Harbin Museum of Architecture and Art. The original St. Sophia's was a wooden structure built in 1907; it was replaced by a brick structure in 1912. The current building is an imposing stone church laid out in the shape of a cross with a large dome, multiple spires, and an imposing bell tower. During the Cultural Revolution it was used as a warehouse but was mercifully undamaged in its utility.

There are seven bronze bells that hang in the bell tower of St. Sophia's; these are clearly visible from the square that surrounds the church. Unfortunately, no amount of pleading and persuading and cudgeling on my part could persuade the people on duty in the museum to let us into the tower to get a closer look at the bells.

Even though Russian Orthodoxy is not recognized as one of China's official legal religions, its presence in China dates back to the late 1600's. The first Orthodox Christians in China were taken captive when the forces of the Qing emperor Kangxi captured their fortress on the Amur River in 1685. There were forty-five prisoners, one of whom was an Orthodox priest named Father Maxim Liontev. He was taken with the other prisoners to Beijing, where he was eventually allowed to take up residence in the Russian embassy. He established a chapel in an old temple on the site and from there he ministered to the faithful. The church was consecrated in 1695; Father Liontev passed away in 1712.

Shortly thereafter, the Russian government established a permanent Orthodox Mission in China, which served both diplomatic and religious functions. Since their activities were restricted to

Beijing, by 1860 there were only two hundred Orthodox believers in China, most of whom were descendants of the prisoners who had arrived in 1685.

In many ways, the growth of the Orthodox Mission in China closely paralleled that of the Protestant missions movement. With the signing of the Treaty of Tianjin in 1858, which required China to allow foreigners to reside in regions of the country outside of Beijing and Shanghai, the church began to spread to other parts

The Ukranian Orthodox Church in Harbin, Heilongjiang Province

of the country. By 1900 there were Orthodox churches in Hankou along the Yangtze River, and Zhangjiakou just outside of Beijing. When the Boxer Rebellion broke out that year, Orthodox Christians suffered along with Protestants and Catholics. Two hundred Orthodox believers were killed and their churches burned. This trial led not to death, but growth: two years later there were 6,000 members.

Because of the increase in the number of Russians in Harbin, the diocese was established in 1912. It remained a part of the Russian Orthodox Church Outside of Russia, the official name of the diaspora church for many years, until 1949, when jurisdiction of all Orthodox Christians transferred to China. In 1956 the last Russian bishop departed, leaving behind 20,000 believers. To this day there is still no formal recognition of the Orthodox Church in China.

The formal name of this particular church is The Church of the Holy Protection of the Mother of God. Although the current structure dates to 1930, the congregation was established in 1922 as the Ukrainian Parish. In the early days of the parish, the congregation met in a home, but by 1930 had grown enough to need its own building. The new church was built on the grounds of the Russian Cemetery, which served as the final resting place for many of the city's Russian residents.

We arrived at the church that Sunday morning with hopes running high because we had some *guanxi*, that is, relationship currency that might get us access to the church bell. Chinese society is built upon a complex web of relationships (*guanxi*). More than simply being bound together by emotional bonds, relationships in Chinese culture are bound together and linked to outsiders by a complex web of favors and transferred trust. Friends help friends, and friends help friends of friends. In this case the *guanxi* net had taken on a decidedly international flavor. An American friend of ours had some Russian friends who worshiped at the church. They knew the Chinese man in charge of the church and had my American friend to tell us that we should meet them there on Sunday morning. Their willingness to help us was rooted in their trust of our American friend and we were hoping that since the Chinese man in charge of the church trusted them, he would also trust us.

We met the Russians in front of the church before the service began, introducing ourselves and trying to explain why we were interested in seeing the bell and learning about the church. Serge, a jolly fellow with a salt-and-pepper beard, seemed to us to be some sort of leader within the Russian community in Harbin. Like many Russians in the city today, he ran a trading company. He was also very knowledgeable about the Russian heritage of Harbin.

The church has the distinction of being the only functioning Russian Orthodox Church in China; it is opened for one hour on Sunday mornings so that the descendants of Russian settlers and Russians living in the city now can have a place to worship. There is no priest. Father Zhu, who had been the last remaining Orthodox priest in China, died in 2000.

In 1989 the *Chicago Tribune* published an article about Father Zhu and his congregation:

> *Father Zhu has never been to the Soviet Union. Born into a family of Chinese converts, he was ordained in Beijing by the last of the Russian expatriate popes. "I am the only Russian Orthodox Priest in China, and this is the only Russian Orthodox church in the country," he said with some pride.*[17]

At that time his congregation numbered perhaps 200, with less than half of them being descendants of the "White Russians," Czar loyalists who fled to China after the Bolshevik Revolution. Writing about the church and its icons and relics, the author says,

> *He lost them temporarily during the Cultural Revolution when*

---

17. Uli Schmetzer, "A Russian Church Hangs on in China," *Chicago Tribune*, (April 28, 1989), accessed September 18, 2016, http://articles.chicagotribune.com/1989-04-28/news/8904080088_1_russian-orthodox-bolshevik-revolution-harbin.

the infamous Red Guards carted off the church icons and religious paintings, the sacred chalices and the triptych to the local museums. They turned the church into a warehouse for books and later into their "Bureau for Culture."[18]

As we were milling around the church before the service,

The bell in the Orthodox Church

chatting with our new Russian friends, an older Chinese woman came out with a small bag of cookies in her hand. She came over to where we were standing and offered some to us.

"It's been twelve years since our last priest passed away," she said. "Here, eat a cookie to honor his memory."

A little puzzled, but also a bit hungry, we each took one. The Russians told us that it is a tradition to eat something in commemoration of the death of special people. They graciously asked Amy

18. Ibid.

and me to join them in remembering their departed priest. We could not have been more honored.

The service ended around 11:30 a.m. and then the work began as we set about trying to get permission to go up into the bell tower. Since our new Russian friends were the ones with the relationship to the leader of the church, we were content to hang back and let them do the talking.

"Only speak when we ask you to," Serge said. "And whatever you do, don't tell him that you are American Protestants!"

After a fruitless conversation that lasted for a few minutes, he gave me the signal, calling me in to make the final appeal, directly and in Chinese. I told the man that I viewed the bell as a symbol of God's love for the Chinese church and that I wanted to tell that story. Upon hearing that, he asked me to write down my contact information. At least if something went wrong, he would know who I was and how to tell the police to find me! He then took out his keys and opened the door to the tower. The guanxi net had held together. Fortunately he didn't ask me about either my nationality or my religion.

Our parade of Russian worshippers and two crazy Americans followed the leader up the stairs. The Chinese women ushers decided they too wanted to see the bell, so they joined us in the climb. At first they tried to prevent us from taking pictures, but relented after we persuaded them we needed photos for our research.

Even though the inscriptions on the bell were in old Russian, our friends were able to tell us that it had been cast in Moscow in 1899 and that it weighed 784 kilograms (1,728 pounds).

It is not clear what happened to the bell during the Cultural Revolution. One elderly parishioner we talked to remembered a time when it just sat on the ground outside of the church, perhaps too big and strong to move and burn. An American friend of mine who lived in Harbin in the 1980's remembers hearing it rung on occasion.

We were certainly excited that we got up to see the bell, but the Russians felt the thrill even more since it was their cultural and religious heritage we were glimpsing. They were also happy to meet a couple of nutty Americans who were not only interested in that heritage, but wanted to tell others about it.

After seeing the bells and offering our thanks to the church staff, we went out to celebrate with our Russian friends. As we enjoyed a wonderful meal together—with Chinese as the common language among us—I couldn't help thinking that, given the circumstances of our seeing it, the message that rings forth from this bell is the message of that great hymn, "In Christ There Is No East or West," which first appeared in an English-language hymnal in 1931:[19]

> *In Christ there is no east or west,*
> *in Him no south or north;*
> *But one great fellowship of love*
> *throughout the whole wide earth.*
> *In Him shall true hearts everywhere*
> *their high communion find;*
> *His service is the golden cord*
> *close binding all mankind.*
> *Join hands then, members of the faith,*
> *whatever your race may be;*
> *Who serves my Father as a child*
> *is surely kin to me.*
> *In Christ now meet both east and west,*
> *in Him meet south and north;*
> *All Christly souls are one in Him*
> *throughout the whole wide earth.*

---

19. Michael C. Hawn, "In Christ There Is No East or West," Discipleship Ministries, accessed July 1, 2016, http://www.umcdiscipleship.org/resources/history-of-hymns-in-christ-there-is-no-east-or-west.

Seven months after we visited the church an historic event took place there. His Holiness Patriarch Kirill of Moscow and All Russia celebrated the Divine Liturgy at the church on May 14, 2013. The Patriarch, who is the head of the Russian Orthodox Church, was in the country on an official visit that included meeting the Chinese president. Many in the Harbin Russian community were in attendance, and when I looked at photos online I spotted some of the kind souls, Chinese and Russian, who had helped us see the bell. I couldn't help wondering if they had rung the bell. I hope so because if they had, the message it pealed would have been the same as the message of the service: God is faithful.

Bells in the Church
Bells in the Bible

Even though bells have been closely associated with churches and worship rituals of Christianity, there are surprisingly few mentions of bells in the Bible. The first reference is in Exodus 28, where God is giving instructions to the Israelites regarding the priestly garments:

> *You shall make the robe of the ephod all of blue. It shall have an opening for the head in the middle of it, with a woven binding around the opening, like the opening of a garment, so that it may not tear. On its hem you shall make pomegranates of blue and purple and scarlet yarns, around its hem, with bells of gold between them, a golden bell of pomegranate, around the hem of the robe. And it shall be on Aaron when he ministers, and its sound shall be heard when he goes into the Holy Place before the LORD, and when he comes out, so that he does not die. (Exodus 28:31-35 ESV)*

In this passage the bells seem to be providing protection as well as announcing the priest's entrance into the temple. In the Russian

Orthodox Church they still attach bells to the vestments of the Hierarchs, although they do not ascribe protective qualities to them.[20]

The next time we see a reference to a bell is in the last chapter of Zechariah, on the horses riding forth on the Day of the Lord. After describing the Day of the Lord and what will befall the nations that come against Israel, the prophet says, "And on that day there shall be inscribed on the bells of the horses, 'Holy to the Lord.'" (Zechariah 14:20 ESV). Not only are there bells on the horses, but they have inscriptions on them as well.

On July 7, 1861, Charles Spurgeon commented in the introduction to a sermon on this text:

> *What connection there may be between that day and others which I have mentioned it is not my purpose this morning to explain. I would that this were to us personally the day when it should be fulfilled in us as individuals, and may the Lord hasten the happy day when universally throughout the Church this text shall be fulfilled, and upon the bells of the horses there shall be "Holiness unto the Lord."*[21]

He goes on to note the difficulty in translating the Hebrew word for bells:

> *The original Hebrew word translated "bells" is a very singular one, because nobody knows precisely what it means. The fact is, the Hebrews knew so little of horses from being interdicted from their use that they had not a very large vocabulary to describe the harness and other equipments of the horse. The word is translated by some critics, "bells," by others, "bits," by some "frontlets," by others "collars," by*

---

20. Andrew Gould, "Bell Ringing in Scripture and Literature," from BLAGOVEST BELLS, *Orthodox Arts Journal*, September 3, 2013, http://www.orthodoxartsjournal. org/bell-ringing-in-scripture-and-liturgy-from-blagovest-bells/.

21. Charles Spurgeon, "A Peal of Bells," *Bible Hub*, accessed September 18, 2016, http://biblehub.com/library/spurgeon/spurgeons_sermons_volume_7_1861/a_peal_ of_bells.htm.

Bells in the Church

some, and by Calvin especially, "blinkers," and Calvin hints that the word may mean "stables." The words must then mean—"the furniture of the horses shall be, 'Holiness unto the Lord,'" and there is no doubt a comparison between the horses and the High Priest.[22]

Then, turning to a summation of the application of this text, he says,

> *The simple meaning of the text is just this, that the day shall come when in common life holiness shall be the guiding star, when the ordinary actions of human existence shall be as much the worship of God as the sacrifice of the altar of mission of the high priest when he went within the veil. Everything, that which was most despised—the horses, the places seemed most likely to be consecrated—the stables, and those things which seemed to be the least holy, even the horses' harness—all shall be so thoroughly used in obedience to God's will that everywhere there shall be "Holiness unto Jehovah." Common things, then, in the day spoken of by Zechariah, are to be dedicated to God and used in his service. I shall work out this great thought in a somewhat novel manner. First let us hear the horses' bells; secondly, let us commend their music; and then, thirdly, let us go home and tune our bells, that they may be in harmony with this sacred chime—"Holiness unto the Lord!"*[23]

The word "cymbal" in the English Bible can also be thought of as a bell. Unlike the ornamental bells affixed to the priests' garments and the horses, a cymbal was actually a musical instrument used during services in the Temple and Tabernacle.

In the Old Testament there are numerous references to their use in worship, including this familiar one from Psalm 150: "Praise him with sounding cymbals, praise him with loud clashing cymbals." (Psalm 150:5 ESV)

22. Ibid.
23. Ibid.

In the New Testament Paul is the only one to reference a cymbal, and leave it to him to put a negative spin on it all! Writing to the church in Corinth, he says, "If I speak in the tongues of men and of angels, but have not love, I am a noisy gong or a clanging cymbal." (1 Corinthians 13:1 ESV)

We know, then, that bells and cymbals were used in ancient Jewish rituals of worship, at least until the destruction of the Temple. We do not see their use in Christian worship in the New Testament. How, then, did they come to have such prominence in the life of the Church throughout the ages?

A History of Bells in Christianity

Catholic tradition has it that the first time bells would have been heard in a church was in the Roman city of Nola, near modern-day Naples. Saint Paulinus, the Bishop of Nola, initially used them to call the monks to worship. Pope Sabinianus approved them to call parishioners to Mass in the seventh century, and in the eighth century they were being used at Requiem Masses. By the ninth century, bells were being rung from churches in towns and hamlets all over the Roman Empire.

Writing in the March 2005 edition of *Adoremus Bulletin*, Matthew D. Herrara explains in greater detail the use of these "sanctus bells:"

> *It wasn't until the thirteenth century that outdoor tower bells began to be rung as "Sanctus Bells" during Mass. It is interesting to note that tower bells are still used today as Sanctus Bells at the Basilica of St. Peter in the Vatican and a great many other historic churches and cathedrals...*
>
> *These tower bells were rung at the consecration and presentation of the Eucharist. First and foremost, the Sanctus Bells were rung during the Mass to create a joyful noise to the Lord, often in conjunction with*

the select musical instruments such as the lyre, as described in Psalm 98:4: "Make a joyful noise to the Lord, all the earth; break forth into joyous song and sing praises." (ESV)

Ringing the bells also gave notice to those unable to attend Mass (the sick, slaves, outside guards) that something divine and miraculous was taking place inside the church building. The voice of the bell would allow people to stop what they were doing to offer an act of adoration to God. Additionally, the bells helped focus the attention of the faithful inside the church on the miracle that was taking place on the altar of sacrifice.[24]

After the Reformation, the newly formed Protestant churches kept the custom of bell ringing, not as a part of the service, but primarily as a means to call the faithful to worship.

Bell use came later in the Orthodox Church. While there is evidence of bells being used in Latin churches in Constantinople by the tenth century, in the Greek Church they continued to use a wooden plank and hammer instrument called the semantron. According to Natali Ashanin, writing in an article at the Russian Orthodox site *Theologic*:

It is said that the semantron, which some monasteries have named "Adam," goes all the way back to Noah, who used it to call the animals to the ark. Just as the ark was the means of salvation from the flood, so the Church is the means of salvation from sin, and church bells call us to our salvation just as semantron did in Noah's time. Following the Greek custom, the first Russian churches and others used these wooden or iron boards, until later bells were introduced.[25]

---

24. Matthew D. Herrera, "Sanctus Bells: Their History and Use in the Catholic Church," *Adoremus Bulletin*, (March 2005), http://www.adoremus.org/0305SantusBells.html.
25. Natalie Ashanin, "All About Bells," *Theologic.com*, accessed September 18, 2016, http://www.theologic.com/oflweb/forkids/bells.htm.

Inscriptions

Many of the bells we found had some sort of inscription on them. This would have been in keeping with a custom that appears to have begun in the fourteenth century. The earliest inscriptions were quite simple, usually the name of a saint or a simple phrase, and often in the first person, as if the bell itself were speaking. [26]

"The Bells of Blessed Paul"
"In Honor of Saint Lawrence"

Occasionally the inscription included the name of the founder.[27]

"Michael de Wymbis made me"
"Jon cast me"

Later, it was popular for the inscription to be an invocation to a saint.[28]

"Saint Katherine, pray for us"

Then there are the rhyming hexameter verses, called "leonines."[29]

"I am called the Bell of Mary, the Excellent Virgin"
"I have the name of heaven-sent Gabriel"

It was also common to include texts of Scripture, particularly in the seventeenth century.[30]

---

26. H. G. Walters, *Church Bells*, (London: A. R. Mowbray & Co. Ltd., 1908), Kindle location 749.
27 Ibid.
28 ibid.
29 ibid., location 757
30 ibid., locoation 770

"Blessed be the Name of the Lord"
"Jesus of Nazareth, King of the Jews"

Inscription on one of the bells
in the Xishiku Catholic Church in Beijing

Following the Reformation in England, there was a shift in the nature of inscriptions on bells, to signify the church's break with Rome. Sometimes they even had a bit of cheek.

One bell from the 1600's, in perhaps a dig at the Catholic custom of praying for the dead, proclaims, "I sound not for the souls of the dead but for the ears of the living." Another bell made in 1678 bears a more direct and biting inscription: "Lord, by thy might keep us from Pope and Hypocrite."[31]

Whatever the inscription, it is clear that the ringing of the bell was a means of communication, either invoking God himself, the saints, or sounding forth a message to all who might hear.

---

31. Ibid, location 930.

Hymns

In the eighteenth and nineteenth centuries, hymn writers took up the theme of bells in their compositions. Perhaps the words of the hymn "Missionary Bells" was part of the inspiration for the Protestant missionaries of the early twentieth century to take bells with them to China. Eliza Edmunds, a Sunday school teacher in Philadelphia wrote the lyrics in 1915:

Verse 1: Keep them ringing, keep them ringing, missionary bells, / Pealing out the news of Jesus' love; / While our gifts we bring to Jesus, happy music swells, / Telling of our blessed Friend above.

Refrain: Bells! Bells! Missionary bells, / Keep them ringing, keep them ringing, each a story tells; / Sounding loud and free over land and sea, / Keep them ringing, keep them ringing, missionary bells.

Verse 2: Keep them ringing, keep them ringing, let the children's hands / Pull the cords of love and faith and praise, / Till the children now in darkness, hear of God's commands, / Learn to follow in the Savior's ways. [Refrain]

Verse 3: Keep them ringing, keep them ringing, every one may share / In the loving service of our King; / Bring an off'ring, willing off'ring, wrap it up in pray'r; / Help the missionary bells to ring. [Refrain][32]

---

32. E. E. Hewitt, "Missionary Bells," *Hymnary.org,* accessed September 18, 2016, https://www.hymnary.org/hymn/KoK1915/130.

Nangangzi Catholic Church
Beijing

In 2013, the year after traipsing around China looking for bells, I visited my niece in Juneau, Alaska. During my stay we took a drive north out of the city on the only road in the area. It comes to an abrupt end after only forty miles. Along the way we stopped at the Shrine of St. Therese, a Catholic retreat center about fifteen miles out of town.

As we were admiring the gorgeous chapel set in a grove of trees on the tip of a peninsula, I remembered visiting a Shrine to St. Therese of Lisieux before. The previous fall, while hunting for bells in Beijing, I had stumbled across a small Catholic church that is also a shrine to St. Therese of Lisieux.

I had never heard of the Nangangzi Catholic Church until Brother Liu took me there in the fall of 2012. I was sure that we had visited all of the major Catholic churches in the city, but he kept assuring me that there was another one in Nangangzi, a poor industrial district situated within what used to be the "Chinatown" section of Beijing.

To understand why there would be a "Chinatown" in the middle of a city in China, it's important to know that the Qing Dynasty, which lasted from 1644 to 1910, was in effect a foreign occupation of China. The Qing rulers were from Manchuria, and when they occupied Beijing in 1644 one of the things they did was move

The Nangangzi Catholic Church in Beijing

the Chinese out of the inner city, declaring that only Manchurians could live within the city walls. They booted the Chinese to the land immediately outside the southern wall, and then built another wall around that district. It became known as the Outer City, or Chinese City. It was a rough-and-tumble place, known for commerce and carousing.

It was in this part of town that Carmelite missionaries had

built their shrine to St. Therese of Lisieux, a French saint, in 1910. In addition to a church, there had been a convent, an orphanage, and a clinic. Today a beautiful little Catholic church set in a quiet garden remains on the site. The current structure was built in 1923. The church was closed in 1958, and reopened for services again on September 1, 1986.

In keeping with its surrounding environment, the sanctuary of Nangangzi Church is simple: blue pillars supporting a white ceiling and walls. On the wall of the nave behind the altar is a giant painting of St. Therese. As we admired the painting I resolved to learn more about her.

She was born in Alençon, France in January 1873, and died at Lisieux in September 1897. Like four of her eight siblings before her, she longed to join a religious order. She applied to enter the Carmelite Covenant at age fifteen, but was refused for being too young. Not wanting to take no for an answer, she and her father travelled to Rome to make a direct appeal to the Pope. The Pope deferred to the superior of the convent who eventually agreed to allow her to join.

She was only in the order for eleven years before she died, but during that time she wrote a short autobiography. It was published in France two years after she died, and translated and published in English in 1912. According to the online Catholic Encyclopedia New Advent,

Its success was immediate and it has passed into many editions, spreading far and wide the devotion to this "little" saint of simplicity, and abandonment in God's service, of the perfect accomplishment of small duties.

The fame of her sanctity and the many miracles performed through her intercession caused the introduction of her cause of canonization only seventeen years after her death, 10 June, 1914.[33]

---

33. Henri Cordier, "The Church in China," *New Advent*, (New York: Robert Appleton Company, 1908), accessed September 18, 2016, http://www.newadvent.org/cathen/17721a.htm.

There were two small bells in the Nangangzi church steeple that the priest graciously allowed us to see. They were not the

The bells in the Nangangzi Catholic Church

original bells installed in the church, and the priest, who had only been at the church a short time, did not know anything about them. Unfortunately there was nothing on the bells themselves to indicate when and where they were made.

I must admit to being a bit disappointed. There were so many unanswered questions! Had a bell been installed when the church was built? Had it been brought over from France? What had happened to it during the Cultural Revolution?

I also reflected on the fact that even though there are now no westerners connected with this church, at some point it was decided that bells were needed. They were deemed important enough in the life of the church to have new ones cast and placed in the old tower. Perhaps it also had something to do with wanting to stay connected to the Church Universal.

While there are many things I was unable to discover about these bells, one thing remained clear: God's steadfast faithfulness to his Church in China.

Xishiku Catholic Church
Beijing

On a late September afternoon, I and my two fellow intrepid bell hunters Amy and Spring found ourselves in the bell tower of the Xishiku Catholic Cathedral (also known as *Beitang*, the Northern Church) in Beijing. Judging by the amount of dust, we felt certain that we were the first to climb the tower in decades.

The church, one of my favorites in the city, sits in a quiet compound at the end of a lane in one of Beijing's oldest *hutong* districts. Such is the history of this church that in my office I have a map of Beijing in 1900 hanging on the wall, and it is clearly marked.

Established in 1703 by the Jesuits, it was christened The Church of the Savior. The first building was completed in 1723 on land given to the Jesuits by the emperor as a way of expressing gratitude for curing him of malaria. Over the next one hundred and fifty years possession of the church would go back and forth between the Church and the emperor, depending on the court's shifting attitudes toward the Church. By 1890, however, things were better and a new church structure was built: the one that is standing today.

73

In 1900 the Boxer Rebellion, which had been raging in the North China countryside, reached Beijing. The Boxers were the spearhead of an anti-Western, anti-Christian movement that sought to rid China of their ideas. The soldiers were called "boxers" because

Xishiku Catholic Church in Beijing

of the shadow boxing-like movements they made, believing that in doing them they would be able to ward off foreign bullets. During that summer, the Boxers laid siege to the legation quarter, also known as the embassy district, and to Christian churches. Three thousand Christians who had sought refuge there were massacred. Even though the church building was heavily damaged, it was not destroyed. Upon entering the compound and the church, it is hard not to think of the martyrs who lost their lives there just a little more than a hundred years ago.

Earlier in the day Amy, Spring, and I had been to the Bell Museum of Beijing; we had heard that the bell from this church was actually on display in the museum. We found a bell that was labeled as having been in a French church, took a bunch of pictures, and then headed to Xishiku to see if they could verify whether or not the bell in our photos belonged to them.

As I have mentioned before, the first step to getting into any church is getting past the gatekeeper and this was no exception. We were met by a nice lady who, when we explained what we were seeking, told us that we needed to speak to the priest. Fortunately, she was happy to help and took us directly to his office.

Imagine his surprise when two foreign women and a Chinese woman walked into his office and started babbling on about bells. We showed him the pictures we'd taken of the bell in the museum and asked if he could confirm if it was from his church. Since he had only recently been installed at this church, he didn't know. In fact he had never seen, much less thought about, that bell. "But there are still two bells up in the towers," he told us.

"Wait," we said, "there are more bells than the one in the museum?"

"Yes," he said. "They only took one of the bells to the museum; we still have the other two."

That's all we needed to hear for Spring to go into her "I will smile and ask him if we can go up into the tower until I wear him down and he says yes" routine. Fortunately it only took a few minutes for him to relent and direct a young assistant to get his keys and take us up into the tower.

Getting up into the east tower was no easy feat. It involved climbing a very old set of rickety stairs and then up some wobbly ladders onto the platform directly under where a giant bell was hanging. Amy, who is not fond of heights, opted to wait at the bottom of the stairs, holding our backpacks.

Hanging above our heads in the east tower was a bell from Toulouse, France that was cast in 1867 by the French founder Pelegrin, son of Louison. The main inscription was simply "MARIA." The bell we had seen earlier in the day was named "JOSEPH" and was cast in the same foundry in the same year. We had found its twin! Our dauntless guide pointed to the empty space where the bell had hung before being taken to the museum.

These two bells, now separated, had been christened "Joseph" and "Maria" in order to remind us of the family that God chose for the incarnation of his son. And just as Joseph and Mary brought Jesus to the people, so the bells call us to come to Jesus.

But where was the second bell that the priest had mentioned?

It was in the West Tower, which meant in order to see it we would have to climb into the space between the sanctuary ceiling and the roof of the cathedral and crawl across some ancient dust-covered beams. Spring did her best to talk me out of it, fearing that I might fall through the ceiling and land on the parishioners praying in the sanctuary. But I was not to be thwarted; I was determined to see this bell, her pleadings notwithstanding.

We arrived without mishap, much to Spring's relief, and began our examination of the bell. It was much larger and had an inscription indicating that it had been cast in 1900 by Edouard Biron, a founder in Paris. It was named "ST MICHAEL." Since it was also inscribed with the word PEKING, it was most likely specifically cast for use in this church, perhaps in response to learning of the damage to the church during the Boxer Rebellion.

The young assistant told us that the bell we had seen in the museum had been taken rather recently. We gathered by the way he told us about it that the parishioners were none too happy about it. When we asked him what had happened to the bells during the Cultural Revolution, he told us that none of the bells had been removed. Had the Red Guards tried, but failed because the bells were too strong? Perhaps.

The important thing was that the bells had survived, and they and their message are no longer silent.

One of the bells in the Xishiku Catholic Church

Jiangsu Road Church
Qingdao, Shandong Province

In a country where incongruous sightings are a daily occurrence, the sight of a Bavarian-style church on a leafy hill overlooking the coastal city of Qingdao was still a bit jarring. Amy and I had travelled down from Beijing the day before to hunt for bells in the churches of this former German colony.

Qingdao was once under German control and unlike most other former colonial cities in China, many of the old neighborhoods and buildings have been spared the wrecking ball. One of the most prominent of these preserved structures is the Christian Church on Jiangsu Road, which sits on a hill just down the road from the former Governor's mansion.

On a gorgeous Saturday morning, Amy and I walked down the street from our hotel just behind the Governor's Mansion to visit the church. Our goal was simple: to talk our way into the bell tower and see the bell. As is the case with most enterprises in China, the church sits within a walled and gated compound. As we walked up a driveway towards the gate, a middle-aged woman stopped us and directed us to the ticket window just outside the gate.

The reason there is an entrance fee is because, even though the church still functions as a place of worship for Christians in Qingdao, it is also a tourist site, under the management of the city's Tourism Bureau. We weren't opposed to purchasing tickets but

The Jiangsu Road Church in Qingdao, Shandong Province

before doing so, I decided to tell my story to the smiling lady in hopes that she might direct us to the right person who could help us see the bell.

"We are Christians from America," I said, "but we now live in Beijing. We are researching the history of churches in China and are particularly interested in old church bells. Your church is very famous and we want to see it. If possible, we would like to talk to someone who can tell us about the bell in your church. Perhaps you can help us."

The phrase I used to ask for help was *bang mang*, which is best translated as "do a favor," or "help out." I call it the "dreaded *bang mang*" because once it's been put out there, it is almost impossible to refuse, particularly if there is some sort of relationship between the speakers. If a person asks a close friend to *bang mang* there is practically no way to say no.

The woman's face lit up. "You are sisters! Wonderful!" On the surface it may seem that we did not have a relationship, close or otherwise, with the woman at the gate. However, the fact that we identified ourselves as Christians meant that we could now refer to each other as "sisters." Her motivation to help us was now rooted in a relationship, not of blood, but of a shared faith.

She directed the other woman to take us, the American sisters, into the church office to meet Mr. Wang. She smilingly assured us that we did not have to buy any tickets; they were for tourists, not sisters.

Upon entering the church compound we had to run the gauntlet of wedding photo shoots that had set up shop on a gorgeous Saturday morning. Wedding photos are taken very seriously in China and are usually done weeks or even months in advance of the actual wedding. Costing into the thousands of dollars, and including multiple changes of clothes and venues, couples are herded around town from scenic spot to scenic spot searching for that perfect shot. And even though most of the couples would consider themselves to be atheists, having a wedding photo taken in front of a church is an absolute must. The Jiangsu Road Christian Church is one of the most popular spots to take wedding photos.

Having made our way through all the couples and photographers, trying as best we could to stay out of the shots, we were ushered into the church office, a gorgeous wood-paneled room that seemed like something straight out of Masterpiece Theater. The sister who was escorting us introduced us to Mr. Wang, a dapper sunglasses-wearing dude who was the keeper of the bells.

"Please take these sisters up to see the bells," she said.

Apparently thinking that it was the most natural thing in the world to be directed to take two Americans up into the bell tower, he grabbed his flashlight and wad of keys and said, "Follow me." In China, he who is the keeper of the keys has power and access, and judging by the size of this wad of keys, Mr. Wang was pretty much in charge of the church.

We climbed three stories into the steeple to a landing below where the church's three bells were hung. Unlike previous bells we had seen, these were connected to a mechanical clock, which was situated on this landing. Mr. Wang stopped to tell us the story of this clock, which was intertwined with the story of the city.

This bell and clock apparatus was built specifically for this church building. Qingdao was a German colony from 1898 to 1914. Germany had gained possession of the city as part of an agreement that was forced upon the Qing rulers in retaliation for the murder of two Germans in Shandong province.

Although the German presence in the city was rather short-lived, they nevertheless left their mark, building a railroad, harbor, and shipyards. They also brought beer making to North China, with the opening of the Germania Brewery in 1903. It is still operating today under the name of Tsingtao Beer, the company choosing to still use the traditional Romanization.

Upon taking possession of what was then little more than a fishing village, the Germans quickly put forth and implemented an extensive plan for urban development, which included dividing the city into different zones, each with its own function and emphasis: industry, fishing, education, etc. One zone was designated the European Zone and Chinese were forbidden to live there. It was in this zone that they constructed for themselves a German city, complete with wide, leaf-shaded streets and German-style buildings. Life in the colony was much like other colonial outposts, with the Germans and Chinese living parallel lives. In later years however, there was much more intermingling as the residential restrictions were lifted and joint Chinese-German schools were established.

Work began on the church, designed by German architect Curt

Rothkegal in 1908, and was completed in 1910. Carl John Voskamp, a German missionary with the Lutheran Church Missouri Synod and member of the church, commissioned the bells. He died in Qingdao in 1937 and was buried in a Christian cemetery there. During the Cultural Revolution Red Guards ransacked the cemetery and smashed the headstones. During our little tour, Mr. Wang told us that a few years previous someone had found them and thought

The bell/clock mechanism in the Jiangsu Road Church

they should be taken to the church. The remains of these head-stones are now kept in the bell tower of the church.

The Wuele Foundry in the town of Bockenem, Germany produced the bells and clock specifically for this church. Founded in 1836, it was a major producer of bells in Germany until its closing in 1966.

According to an article in the *Shenzhen Daily News*, a descendent of the owner of a company that supplied gears to J. F. Wuele visited the church in 2009:

The Bells Are Not Silent

When the German businessman Herion visited Qingdao with his 80-year-old father last year, they were attracted by a big clock in a Christian church on Jiangsu Road. The logo of the clock was "J. F. Weule," which was the logo for a German family. About 100 years ago, Weule was famous for making clocks for churches in Germany. "At that time, my family was the gear supplier of the Weule," Herion said. The father and son spent more than a half year to confirm that the gear of the clock in the church on Jiangsu Road was from their ancestors' hands. "I am so proud that my great-great-grandfather's gear is still in great condition after 100 years and I think it can keep working for another 300 years," he said.[34]

Today the bells are still rung every Sunday morning at 9:25 a.m., just before the start of the worship service.

When we asked Mr. Wang how the bell had survived the Cultural Revolution, he said that it had, in fact, never left the building. Following the closure of the church, a nearby university took over the church building and used it as their dining hall. By the time things got really bad, a local unit of the People's Liberation Army (PLA) had occupied the church so the Red Guards didn't dare come in to destroy it.

In other words, the bell was saved by the PLA!

---

34. Yuanyuan Wang, "Clock Works for A Hundred Years," *Shenzhen Daily*, (March 15, 2011), accessed September 18, 2016, http://szdaily.sznews.com/html/2011-03/15/content_1479166.htm.

St. Paul's Church
Qingdao, Shandong Province

Amy and I slipped quietly into the pew at the old St. Paul's Church in Qingdao, now known simply as Guanxiang Road Christian Church. An usher, who for some reason was dressed in a gleaming white suit that seemed more suitable for a night out in Las Vegas than a Chinese church, spotted us, smiled, and came over to where we were sitting.

Uh-oh, I thought. *He's going to ask us to leave.*

"Aren't you the two ladies who were here yesterday asking about the old church bell?" he asked, with a big smile on his face. "Come with me. I'll ask someone to take you up in the tower to see the bell right now."

We looked at each other in bewilderment. On the previous afternoon when we had stopped by the church to inquire about their bell, this very man had treated us with suspicion (Wouldn't you, if two strange foreigners came looking for something so unusual?) and told us that if we wanted to know anything about the church we had to first go to the municipal church office. There had been two other women in the office with him who had tried to adopt a more friendly tone to our requests, but he had simply ordered them not to speak with us. We had left the church feeling disappointed and not a little annoyed with him. Yet here he was, all smiles and eager to help!

We suggested that we would be happy to wait until after the service but he was insistent that we follow him now. He introduced us to another usher and said to her, "These American friends are here to learn about our church and our bell. Please take them up into the tower to see it."

St. Paul's Church in Qingdao, Shandong Province

As the parishioners were making their way into the sanctuary, we climbed up into the gorgeous Romanesque bell tower, our dashed hopes of yesterday being rekindled with every step.

We hadn't even known about this church in Qingdao until the usher/tour guide/historian at the Jiangsu Road Church had told us about it the day before.

"You should go up the street to St. Paul's Church," he had told us. "They have an old bell." Our interest piqued, we had agreed to try, the unexpected detour promising in its potential.

St. Paul's Church

Compared to the other churches we'd visited, this one was relatively new. Construction began in 1938 and was completed in 1941. While the Jiangsu Road Church had been built during the time Qingdao was a colony, St. Paul's Church was built at the beginning of Japan's second occupation of the city. Because Japan and Germany were allies at the time, it is not surprising that there was still a sizeable enough German population in the city to warrant the construction of another church. The architect was W. George Yourieff, a Russian-born Frenchman who lived in China for twenty-five years. He later emigrated to the United States and became a prominent architect in Palo Alto, California.[35]

So here we were, climbing up into the steeple of a Romanesque church building designed by a Russian-French architect for a German congregation in a Chinese city under Japanese occupation!

According to the self-appointed guide at the other church, the bell had been taken away during the Cultural Revolution and installed in a factory in another city in the province, where it was used to mark the beginning and end of work shifts. A worker at the factory from Qingdao recognized that it was from the church and managed to extricate it and hide it away in a storeroom. How a person goes about hiding a giant bell remains something of a mystery. Surely he had help. Somehow the bell had resurfaced in the last few years, and in 2011, the church had purchased it at auction.

As we reached the top of the stairs we caught sight of this bell, which had been lost but was now found.

The inscriptions were in German, so we couldn't read them; however we could make out the date: 1883. I took a photo of the inscription and later sent it to a friend of mine in the U. S., an amateur genealogist who has learned to read enough German to trace his family history. He sent the translations back to me within ten minutes:

---

35. "W. George Yourieff, Prominent Local Architect." *Palo Alto Online.* Last modified July 28, 1999. Accessed September 18, 2016. http://www.paloaltoonline.com/weekly/morgue/community_pulse/1999_Jul_28.OBITLEAD.html

The Bells Are Not Silent

Bochumer Verein Gusstahlfabrik
(Bochumer Union Cast Steel Factory)
Der Gerechte Wird Seines Glaubens Leben
("The righteous shall live by faith")
1883

Founded in 1844, the Bochumer Union Cast Steel Factory was once one of Germany's largest steel mill and mining companies. In addition to casting bells, they made steel for railroads and armaments during the First and Second World Wars.[36] Its most famous bell was the Olympic Bell cast for the 1936 Olympics in Berlin. Inscribed on that bell is the Brandenburg Gate flanked by two Nazi emblems. Along the bottom are the words "I call the youth of the world."

In 1945 the British army took control of the Olympic complex and turned it into their military headquarters. In 1947, fearing the stability of the tower that housed the bell, British engineers blew it up. The bell came crashing down, never to be rung again. Today it is on display outside the Olympic stadium in Berlin.[37]

The phrase inscribed on the bell in St. Paul's Church, "the righteous shall live by faith," is from Romans 1:17. Paul, writing to the believers in Rome, states the source of his confidence: "For I am not ashamed of the gospel, for it is the power of God for salvation to everyone who believes, to the Jew first and also to the Greek. For in it the righteousness of God is revealed from faith to faith, as it is written, 'the righteous shall live by faith.'" It was the truth of these words that gripped the heart and mind of Martin Luther in 1513, and would later lead to the Great Reformation.

36. "Index to carillons and chimes by Bochumer Verein," *Tower Bells.*,accessed September 18, 2016, http://www.towerbells.org/data/IXfoundryBochum.html.
37. Geoff Walden, "Berlin—Reichssportfeld and 1936 Olympics Site." *Third Reich in Ruins*, (July 20, 2000), accessed September 18, 2016, http://www.thirdreichruins.com/olympic.htm.

Writing of its discovery, Luther said, "At last meditating day and night, by the mercy of God, I began to understand that the righteousness of God is that through which the righteous live by a gift of God,

The bell in St. Paul's Church

namely by Faith. Here I felt as if I were entirely born again and had entered paradise itself through the gates that had been flung open."[38] Given the fact that this bell had been cast for a Lutheran church, we were not surprised to see this inscription. Its powerful message of faith remained, unmarred.

---

38. Mark Galli and Ted Oleson, "Martin Luther: Passionate Reformer," *Christianity Today*, accessed September 18, 2016, http://www.christianitytoday.com/history/people/theologians/martin-luther.html.

After taking a few pictures of the bell we hurried back to the sanctuary, taking our seats among the congregation. At 9:25, five minutes before the start of the morning worship service, our friend in the white suit tugged on the weathered rope to ring the bell, each ring announcing to the neighborhood and to the city the truth of that inscription.

The bell in Berlin and the bell in Qingdao, both cast in the same foundry, survived the ravages of war and political turmoil. However, only one is not silent: the one with the message of the Gospel.

Epilogue

At the end of 2012 I moved back to the United States, so "bell-hunting"—getting out to look for more bells—has been suspended for a time. However, the lessons of the bells continue. Bells may seem like ordinary artifacts, ancient or modern, but in fact they are vehicles of history, reminding us that it is alive and accessible in the people, places, and things that surround us. For me, they illuminated stories that were hidden in plain sight. Learning history is about discovering these stories.

The bells also continue to declare that God is faithful to his church, something that I reflect on whenever I see or hear a church bell. In China, God has demonstrated his faithfulness by not only allowing the church to survive, but to thrive and grow. When the Communists came to power in 1949 there were approximately 700,000 Protestant Christians, but by 1979, after two decades of persecution, that number had grown to 10 million. Today conservative estimates place the number at 70 million, with more than 10 million Catholics.

Shortly before moving back to the United States, I had the

opportunity to share these bell stories with a group of Christians in Beijing. At the end, many of them were in tears. "We know so little about the history of the church in China," they said. "This is so encouraging."

A friend who worked in China in the early 1980's, even before I did, told me recently about his memory of seeing an old abandoned church bell on the grounds of the US embassy in Beijing in 1983. He remembers the inscription vividly:

> *Ring out the darkness in the land;*
> *Ring in the Christ that is to be."*

Over the years, political upheaval and modernization have silenced many church bells in China. What cannot be silenced, however, is the truth that God is faithful. That truth continues to be proclaimed by the bells that are not silent.

Do You Know of Other Bells?

My first thought upon discovering the first bell remains: if there is one bell, there must be hundreds of bells around China, each with a voice and a story. If you know of any church bells in China, I would love to hear about them. Please contact me via my website www.joannpittman.com.

Acknowledgements

I would like to thank the following people for their encouragement and assistance in discovering and telling these stories:

Noël Piper, for including me in your adventure to discover the story of Esther Nelson, which led me to the stories of the bells.

Ben, for making connections, opening doors, and driving us around Sichuan. Your help and insights were invaluable.

Amy, for your partnership in finding many of these bells and your nagging to get this book written.

Spring and Jessie, for enthusiasm in translating both written and spoken stories.

Julia, for being a wonderful editor; for taking my disjointed stories, giving them structure, and tying them together.

To numerous friends and family members who never stopped encouraging me to get this done.

Bibliography

刘豪杰. "Orthodox Christianity in Harbin." Ecumenical Buddhism, Daoism, & Confucianism. Last modified October 1, 2011. Accessed September 6, 2016. http://ecumenicalbuddhism. blogspot.ca/2011/10/orthodox-christianity-in-harbin.html.

Admin. "Patriarch Kirill celebrated Divine Liturgy at Intercession Church in Harbin," Pravmir.com: Orthodox Christianity of the World. Last modified May 16, 2013. Accessed September 6, 2016. http://www.pravmir.com/patriarch-kirill-celebrated-divine-liturgy-at-intercession-church-in-harbin/.

"Age-old Chinese Bell Culture, The." China.org.cn. Accessed September 6, 2016. http://www.china.org.cn/english/ features/FbiCh/78450.htm.

Ashanin, Natalie. "All About Bells." Theologic.com. Accessed September 6, 2016. http://www.theologic.com/oflweb/ forkids/bells.htm.

Bibliography

Avgerinos. "Orthodoxy in China." Orthodox Christian Comment. Accessed September 6, 2016. http://www.orthodox-christian-comment.co.uk/news-orthodoxy_in_china.htm.

Batuman, Elif. "The Bells: How Harvard Helped Preserve a Russian Legacy." The New Yorker. Last modified April 27, 2009. http://www.newyorker.com/magazine/2009/04/27/the-bells-6.

Bays, Daniel. A New History of Christianity in China. Massachusetts: Wiley-Blackwell, 2012.

B. C. "Orthodox Christianity in China: A Comb Worth Fighting For." The Economist. Last modified October 31, 2014. Accessed September 6, 2016. http://www.economist.com/blogs/erasmus/2014/10/orthodox-christianity-china.

Bell, Birdie. "The Old Church Bell," Hymnary.org. Accessed September 18, 2016. https://www.hymnary.org/hymn/TS51896/18.

"Bell Tower of Berlin Olympic Stadium." Wikipedia. Last modified August 6, 2016. Accessed September 6, 2016. https://en.wikipedia.org/wiki/Bell_Tower_of_Berlin_Olympic_Stadium.

"Bells." Medieval Life and Times. Accessed September 7, 2016. http://www.medieval-life-and-times.info/medieval-music/bells.htm.

Benedictine Monks of Buckfast Abbey. "Church Bells." Catholic-Culture.org. Accessed September 6, 2016. http://www.catholicculture.org/culture/library/view.cfm?recnum=3665.

Bibliography

"Bethlehem Baptist Church Archives." Minnesota History Center. Accessed September 7, 2016. http://www2.mnhs.org/ library/findaids/00667.xml.

"Bochum Association for Mining and Cast Steel Manufacturing, The." Jahrhunderthalle Bochum. Accessed September 6, 2016. http://www.jahrhunderthalle-bochum.de/en/ besucher/historie/infotafeln-westpark/der-bochumer-vere-in-fuer-bergbau-und-gussstahlfabrikation.

Charbonnier, Jean. "Catholic Churches in Beijing: South Church." China-Zentrum.de. Accessed September 6, 2016. http:// china-zentrum.de/Churches-in-China.354.0.html?&L=1.

"Church of China." Orthodox Wiki. Last modified August 27, 2013. Accessed September 6, 2016. https://orthodoxwiki. org/Church_of_China.

"Church of Our Lady of Mount Carmel, Beijing." Wikipedia. Last modified August 31, 2016. Accessed September 7, 2016. https://en.wikipedia.org/wiki/Church_of_Our_Lady_of_ Mount_Carmel,_Beijing.

Cincinnati Bell Foundry Company. "Catalogue of the Cincinnati Bell Foundry Co: Cincinnati, Ohio, U.S.A., March 1st, 1889. Successors to the Blymyer Manufacturing Co. in Bells." Google Books. Accessed September 6, 2016. https://books. google.ca/books/about/Catalogue_of_the_Cincinnati_Bell_ Foundry.html?id=XFIftwAACAAJ&redir_esc=y.

Cordier, Henri. "The Church in China." New Advent. New York: Robert Appleton Company (1908). Accessed September 6, 2016. http://www.newadvent.org/cathen/03669a.htm.

Bibliography

Colton. "St. Paul's Church—Qingdao Old Town." ThatsQingdao. com. Last modified September 29, 2009. Accessed September 6, 2016. http://www.thatsqingdao.com/2012/09/qingdao-old-town-st-pauls-church/.

"Death of Rev. C. A. Salquist." Missions: a Baptist Monthly Magazine, Volume 2 (1911): 436-437. https://books.google. com/books?id=dpjNAAAAMAAJ&lpg=PA436&ots=TlX-kn_wLAw&dq=axel%20salquist&pg=PA436#v=onep-age&q=436&f=false.

Donovan, Edith. "St. Thérèse of Lisieux." New Advent. New York: The Encyclopedia Press. Accessed September 6, 2016. http://www.newadvent.org/cathen/17721a.htm.

Editors of Encyclopedia Britannica. "Bell: Musical Instrument." Encyclopedia Britannica. Last modified December 17, 2014. Accessed September 6, 2016. https://www.britannica.com/art/bell-musical-instrument.

Editors of Encyclopedia Britannica. "Zhong: Chinese Bell." Encyclopedia Britannica. Last modified September 28, 2006. Accessed September 6, 2016. https://www.britannica.com/art/zhong.

Erohina, Tatiana. "Growing Up Russian in China: A Historical Memoir." iUniverse. Accessed September 6, 2016. https://books.google.ca/books/about/GROWING_UP_RUSSIAN_IN_CHINA.html?id=KLf1zMCBYRQC&redir_esc=y.

E. W. Vanduzen Co. "Just a Little Bell History." BrosamerBells. com. Accessed September 6, 2016. http://www.brosamers-bells.com/1histpix/vdbellhist.gif.

Bibliography

"Foreign Missionary, The: Containing Particular Accounts of the Work of the Board of Foreign Missions of the Presbyterian Church and Selected Articles and Facts from the Missionary Publications of Other Protestant Societies." Volumes 44-45, Presbyterian Mission House, 1886. Accessed September 7, 2016. https://books.google.ca/books/about/The_Foreign_Missionary.html?id=srEnAAAAYAAJ&redir_esc=y.

Galli, Mark, and Ted Olesen. "Martin Luther: Passionate Reformer." Christianity Today. Accessed September 6, 2016. http://www.christianitytoday.com/history/people/theologians/martin-luther.html.

Goeppinger, Neil. "Buckeye Bell Foundry, VanDuzen & Tift." American Bell. Accessed September 7, 2016. https://americanbell.org/aba-forum/topic/buckeye-bell-foundry-vanduzen-tift/.

Goodson, Caroline and John H. Arnold. "Resounding Community: The History and Meaning of Medieval Church Bells." www.academia.edu. Accessed September 7, 2016. http://www.academia.edu/1431766/_Resounding_Community_The_History_and_Meaning_of_Medieval_Church_Bells_Viator_2010.

Gould, Andrew. "Bell Ringing in Scripture and Literature, from BLAGOVEST BELLS." Orthodox Arts Journal. Last modified September 3, 2013. http://www.orthodoxartsjournal.org/bell-ringing-in-scripture-and-liturgy-from-blagovest-bells/.

Hankey, Kate. "Tell Me the Old, Old Story of Unseen Things Above." Hymnary.org. Accessed September 6, 2016. http://www.hymnary.org/text/tell_me_the_old_old_story_of_unseen_thi.

Bibliography

Hawn, C. Michael. "History of Hymns: 'In Christ There Is No East or West'." Discipleship Ministries. Accessed September 6, 2016. http://www.umcdiscipleship.org/resources/history-of-hymns-in-christ-there-is-no-east-or-west.

Herrera, Matthew D. "Sanctus Bells: Their History and Use in the Catholic Church." Adoremus Bulletin. Last modified March 2005. http://www.adoremus.org/0305SantusBells.html.

"Hidden Churches of Beijing Hutong." China.org.cn. Last modified December 21, 2009. http://www.china.org.cn/travel/2009-12/21/content_19102754.htm.

"Hierarchal Service Is Performed In Harbin's Protection Church for the First Time in a Half Century, A." Proslavie. ru: Orthodox Christianity. Last modified June 24, 2012. Accessed September 6, 2016. http://www.pravoslavie.ru/english/54460.htm.

"History of Columbus Castings." ColumbusCastings.com. Accessed September 6, 2016. http://www.columbuscastings. com/history.html.

"History of Qingdao as a German Colony," Yesterday's Shadow—Colonial Influence on China. Accessed September 7, 2016. https://yesterdaysshadow.wordpress.com/qingdao-germanys-chinese-colony/.

"History of the Bell." The Bell of Honor. Accessed September 7, 2016. http://thebellofhonor.org/about-us/.

Huiguang, Chi. "Christian Church and the Shepherds in Qingdao." China Radio International, Last modified February

Bibliography

26, 2013. Accessed September 7, 2016. http://english.cri. cn/8706/2013/02/26/3262s750549.htm.

"Index to carillons and chimes by Bochumer Verein." Tower Bells. Last modified January 28, 2015. http://www.towerbells.org/ data/IXfoundryBochum.html.

InternChina Admin. "The German History of Qingdao." Intern China™. Last modified March 19, 2013. https://internchina. com/the-german-history-of-qingdao/.

"Ivan the Great Bell Tower." Wikipedia. Last modified July 15, 2016. Accessed September 6, 2016. https://en.wikipedia.org/ wiki/Ivan_the_Great_Bell_Tower.

Ivanova, Vera. "Russian Tradition of Semantron, aka Slavic Flat Bells, Part 1." Russia IC. Last modified June 9, 2015. Accessed September 6, 2016. http://www.russia-ic.com/culture_art/ music/2919/#.VbhHjyTuifQ.

Jewitt, Llewellynn. "Church Bells; Their History, Legends, Superstitions, Uses, &c." Google Books. Accessed September 6, 2016. https://books.google.com/books/about/Church_Bells_their_ history_legends_super.html?id=cCpWAAAAcAAJ.

Lambert, Edie. Millie's China. USA: Promise Publishing Company, 1998.

Lienhard, John H. "Ancient Chinese Bells." Engines of Our Ingenuity. Accessed September 6, 2016. http://www.uh.edu/ engines/epi1676.htm.

Lukianov, Roman. "A Brief History of Russian Bells." Russian-

Bibliography

Bells.com. Accessed September 6, 2016. http://www.russian-bells.com/history/history1.html.

Mao Zedong. "Report to the Second Plenary Session of the Seventh Central Committee of the Communist Party of China." March 5, 1949. Selected Works, Vol. IV, p. 364, Marxists.org, Accessed September 18, 2016. https://www.marxists.org/reference/archive/mao/works/red-book/ch02.htm.

"Ninety-First Annual Report of the American Baptist Missionary Union: 1904-1905." American Baptist Foreign Mission Society. Accessed September 6, 2016. https://books.google.ca/books/about/Annual_Report.html?id=R-WIYAAAAMAAJ&redir_esc=y.

Openshaw, H.J. and William M. Upcraft. "Yachow and Burma: The Escape, the Return." Archive.org. Accessed September 6, 2016. https://archive.org/stream/yachowburmaescap00upcr/yachowburmaescap00upcr_djvu.txt.

Openshaw, H. J. "New Church at Yachow, The." The Journal and Messenger: The Central National Baptist Newspaper, Volume 87, March 7 (1918): 11. https://books.google.com/books?id=tMM7AQAAMAAJ&lpg=PR176&dq=church%20bell%20yachow&pg=PR176#v=onepage&q=church%20bell%20yachow&f=false.

Piper, Noël. "Our 'Following in the Footsteps' Expedition." Tell Me When to Pack. November 16, 2011, accessed July 22, 2016. http://www.tellmewhentopack.com/2011/11/our-following-in-the-footsteps-expedition/.

Pozdniaev, Dionisy. "The Orthodox Church in China: Its

Problems and Prospect." Orthodoxy in China. Accessed September 7, 2016. http://chinese.orthodoxy.ru/english/problems.html.

"Protection (Pokrov) of the Theotokos Church of Harbin." Orthodoxy in China. Accessed September 6, 2016. http://www.orthodox.cn/contemporary/harbin/pokrov_en.htm.

Radev, Igor. "Cossacks—Albazinians in China." Orthodxy in China. Accessed September 6, 2016. http://orthodox.cn/localchurch/19010501razvedchik415-417_en.htm.

Radev, Igor. "The Ukranian Parish." Orthodoxy in China. Accessed September 7, 2016. http://www.orthodox.cn/localchurch/harbin/1931/12-13_en.htm.

Randolph, Bartholomew. "Congregation of Priests of the Mission." New Advent. New York: Robert Appleton Company (1911). Accessed September 6, 2016. http://www.newadvent.org/cathen/10357a.htm.

Rau, Andy. "Ring the Bells of Your Hearts." Bible Gateway. Last modified December 24, 2012. Accessed September 7, 2016. https://www.biblegateway.com/blog/2012/12/ring-the-bells-of-your-hearts/.

Rklawton. "Monk playing a semantron." Wikimedia Commons. Last modified September 16, 2010. https://commons.wikimedia.org/wiki/File:A01_5873.JPG.

"Russian Orthodox Mission in China." Orthodox Wiki. Last modified November 16, 2009. Accessed September 6, 2016. https://orthodoxwiki.org/Russian_Orthodox_Mission_in_China.

Bibliography

Shmetzer, Uli. "A Russian Church Hangs on in China." Chicago Tribune. Last modified April 28, 1989. Accessed September 6, 2016. http://articles.chicagotribune.com/1989-04-28/news/8904080088_1_russian-orthodox-bolshevik-revolution-harbin.

Spurgeon, Charles. "A Peal of Bells." Bible Hub. Accessed September 9, 2016. http://biblehub.com/library/spurgeon/spurgeons_sermons_volume_7_1861/a_peal_of_bells.htm.

"St. Joseph Cathedral (Tianjin)." Wikipedia. Last modified March 31, 2016. Accessed September 6, 2016. https://en.wikipedia.org/wiki/St._Joseph_Cathedral_(Tianjin).

Sullivan, John F. "Church Bells." The East Lewis County Catholic Community. Accessed September 7, 2016. http://www.awakentoprayer.org/church_bells.htm.

"Sunu Case (1724)." Yutopian Online. Accessed September 7, 2016. http://www.yutopian.com/religion/history/Sunu.html.

Thurston, Herbert. "Bells." New Advent. New York: Robert Appleton Company. Accessed September 7, 2016. http://www.newadvent.org/cathen/02418b.htm.

"Tsingtao—A Chapter of German Colonial History in China. 1897–1914." German Historical Museum. Last modified 1998. Accessed September 7, 2016. http://www.dhm.de/archiv/ausstellungen/tsingtau/tsingtau_e.html.

"Value of Church Bells." Brosamer Bells. Accessed September 7, 2016. http://www.brosamersbells.com/1histpix/vdvaluch.gif.

Bibliography

Walden, Geoff. "Berlin—Reichssportfeld and 1936 Olympics Site." Third Reich in Ruins. Last modified July 20, 2000. http://www.thirdreichruins.com/olympic.htm.

Walters, H. B. Church Bells. London: A. R. Mowbray & Co. Ltd., 1908. E-book. Kindle location 888.

Wang, Yuanyuan. "Clock Works for 100 Years," Shenzhen Daily. Last modified March 15, 2011. Accessed September 7, 2016. http://szdaily.sznews.com/html/2011-03/15/content_1479166.htm.

"W. George Yourieff, Prominent Local Architect." Palo Alto Online. Last modified July 28, 1999. http://www.paloaltoonline.com/weekly/morgue/community_pulse/1999_Jul_28.OBITLEAD.html.

Wei, Yan. "A Church Interrupted." Beijing Review. Accessed September 7, 2016. http://www.bjreview.cn/EN/06-22-e/china-5.htm.

"Work of the West China Baptist Mission, The." The West China Missionary News, Volume 39 Number 9 (1937): 1-40. http://images.library.yale.edu/divinitycontent/dayrep/9866641_1937_039-009_eng.pdf.